بِسْمِ اللهِ الرَّحْمَنِ الرَّحِيمِ

THE
ISLAMIC
READER

Islamic Studies for Young People

Mahmood Ibraheem El-Geyoushi

Goodword Books

First published 2002
© Goodword Books 2004
Reprinted 2004

Goodword Books Pvt. Ltd.
1, Nizamuddin West Market
New Delhi 110 013
e-mail: info@goodwordbooks.com
Printed in India

www.goodwordbooks.com

Contents

Preface

As I promised in the first volume of Primary Islamic Teaching to produce a second volume to meet the needs of Muslim students from ages 11 to 16, I feel now that I have fulfilled my promise by producing this volume in order to help young Muslim people to get the necessary knowledge about the religion, belief, worship, morals and the Life of the Prophet as well as the Muslim population in the world.

I tried as much as I could, to make the picture of Islam clear to the young Muslim people who live in this foreign country and are subject to a great deal of pressure from here and there.

It was my aim to let young Muslim understand how rational their religion is and how excellent the life of the Prophet was and the capability of the Muslim way of life for those who want to lead a good life. At the same time to get as much as they want from the modern civilisation as long as this agrees with the Islamic principles.

Also it was my aim to give a chance to our young Muslim brothers in this country to know about the Qur'an and to learn by heart some parts of it as well as the Sunnah of the Prophet. I hope I have reached my aim and I ask Allah, the Almighty, to give benefit to those who read this book and to help me continue serving the religion of Islam.

Muhammad Ibraheem El-Geyoushi

PART 1

BELIEF

CHAPTER 1

The Conception of God in Muslim Belief

Any Muslim in this country could be asked by a non-Muslim what is the concept of God in Islam? And he must be able to give a satisfactory answer.

To give this satisfactory answer you have to know what is the belief of the Muslim in God.

God is One and only One. He has neither children nor partners He is the light of the heavens and of the earth. He knows everything, hears everything and has control over everything. All the universe goes according to His Will He created man and created for him everything that is on the earth, in the sky and everything that is therein. He created the sun, the moon, the stars, and clouds, the mountains and the seas. He made the rain to fall down and the plants to come up out of the earth to provide man his food. All that is in the earth and the sky follows a certain system, which is controlled by the Will of God, the Almighty. God is merciful, generous, the giver of peace and He created death and life. Everything is from Him and will go back to Him. In His hands is dominion and He has power over everything. Him only we worship. From Him only we seek help. Belonging to Him are the most beautiful names as the Holy Qur'an says. God is He, than whom there is no other god. He knows all things, both secret and open. He is Most gracious, Most merciful. God is He, than whom there is no other god. He is The Sovereign, The Holy One, The Source of Peace and Perfection. The Guardian of Faith, The Preserver of Safety, The Exalted in Might, The Irresistible. The Supreme. Glory to God, (High is He) Above the partners, they attribute to Him. He is God, The Creator, The Evolver, The Bestower of forms and colours. To Him belong the Most beautiful names; whatever is in the heavens and on earth declares His praise and glory. And He is The Exalted in Might, The Wise.

In the Holy Qur'an there are many verses dealing with God, His attributes and His actions. God has attributes existing in His which are not He, nor part of Him, but exist in Him and subsist by Him, such as Existence, oneness, Life, Knowledge, Power, Will, Hearing, Sight, Eternity and His Non-Beginning.

THE EXISTENCE OF GOD...

...is absolute, because He is the creator of life and the creator of the whole world and the source of all action. Therefore, His existence must be without doubt. This fact

has been discussed widely in the Holy Qur'an. It is drawn
to the attention of those who denied the existence of God
by showing them the excellence of their creation, as well
as what is around them, in order to awake their hearts
and open their minds, and this is always the way of the
Qur'an when discussing the matter of faith and justifying
the existence of God. Let us hear now the Qur'an deals
with this very point in two places. First in the Chapter of
Believers : - 23/78-92.

It is He who created
For you (the faculties of)
Hearing, sight, feeling
And understanding: little thanks
It is ye give !
And He has multiplied you
Through the earth, and to Him
Shall ye be gathered back.
It is He who gives
Life and death, and to Him
(Is due) the alternation
Of Night and Day :
Will ye not then understand ?
On the contrary they say
Things similar to what
The ancients said.
They say: "What! When we
Die and become dust and bones,
Could we really be
Raised up again ?

"Such things have been promised
To us and to our fathers
Before! They are nothing
But tales of the ancients!"
Say "To whom belong
The earth and all beings therein?
(Say) if ye know!"
They will say, "To God"
Say : 'Yet will ye not
Receive admonition ?
Say "Who is the Lord
Of the seven heavens,
And the Lord of the Throne
(Of Glory) Supreme?
They will say, "(They belong)
To God". Say "Will ye not
Then be filled with awe?
Say: "Who is it in whose
Hands is the governance
Of all things, - who protects
(All), but is not protected
(Of any)? (Say) if ye know.
They will say, "(It belongs)
To God". Say: Then how
Are ye deluded?"
We have sent them the Truth
But they indeed practise Falsehood!
No son did God beget,
Nor is there any god
Along with Him: (If there were

Many gods), behold, each god
Would have taken away
What he had created
And some would have
Lorded it over others!
Glory to God! (He is free)
From the (sort of) things
They attribute to him.
And also in the Chapter of Ants:- (27/59):-
Say : Praise be to God,
And Peace on His Servants
Whom He has chosen
(For His Message). (Who)
Is better? God or
The false gods they associate
(With Him)?
Or, who has created
The heavens and the earth,
And who sends you down
Rain from the sky?
Yea, with it We cause
To grow well-planted orchards
Full of beauty and delight;
It is not in your power
To cause the growth
Of the trees in them. (Can there be
Another) god besides God?
Nay, there are a people
Who swerve from justice.
Or, who has made the earth

Firm to live in; made
Rivers in its midst; set
Thereon mountains immovable;
And made a separating bar
Between the two bodies
Of flowing water ?
(Can there be another) god
Besides God
Or, who listens to the (soul)
Distressed when it calls
On Him, and who relieves
Its suffering, and makes you
(Mankind) Inheritors of the earth ?
(Can there be another) god
Besides God ? Little is
That ye heed.

THE ONENESS OF GOD

God is one and only one because if there were some other gods His control would not be complete and they would fight each other and the arrangement of the world would have collapsed and also He has no partner nor children. The Holy Qur'an says "Say He is God, The One and Only; God, The Eternal, Absolute; He begets not, nor is He begotten; and there is none like unto Him". In another verse, the Holy Qur'an says "God begot no son nor is there any God along with Him. If there were many gods behold each god would have taken away what he had created, and some would have lorded it over others.

Glory to God, He is free from the sort of things attribute to Him".

LIFE

God is alive because if He were not He could not give life to others. The Holy Qur'an says "God! There is no God but He the living the Self-Subsisting Eternal. No slumber can seize Him nor sleep. His are all things in the heavens and the earth. Who is there that can intercede in His Presence except as He permits ? He knows what appears to His creatures as before, or after or behind them, nor shall they compass ought of His knowledge except as He wills. His Throne extends over both the heavens and the earth, and He feels no fatigue in guarding and preserving them, for He is the Most High, the Supreme in Glory.

KNOWLEDGE

God knows everything – what is hidden and what is open. What was spoken out and what was kept in our mind, what is seen and what is unseen, what is on the earth and what is in the sea. Even when a leaf drops from a tree he knows about it. He knows what is inside the earth and whether it is dry or fresh. The Qur'an says "With Him are the keys of the unseen treasure that none knows but He. He knows whatever there is on the earth and in the sea, not a leaf falls but with His knowledge". There is not a grain in the darkness or depth of the earth, nor anything fresh or dry, green or withered, but is inscribed in a record, clear to those who can read. It is He who takes your souls by night and has knowledge of that which you have done by day. When in the day He raises you up again, that a term appointed be fulfilled; In the end, unto Him will be your return. Then will He show you the truth of all that you have done", and the Holy Qur'an says: "It was We who created man and We know what dark suggestions his soul makes to him, for We are nearer to him than his jugular vein".

POWER

The Power of God has no limitations. It is His power that created the universe and controls the delicate arrangement of all that is in either the sky or on earth and keeps it going according to a certain system which, if it were slightly changed, would cause the world to collapse and everything would change. There are many verses in the Holy Qur'an expressing the power of God, such as "Does not man see that it is We who created him from sperm? Yet behold he stands forth as an open adversary and he makes comparisons for Us and forgets his own origin and creation. He says "Who can give life to dry bones and decomposed ones at that ? Say He will give them life who created them for the first time for He is well-versed in every kind of creation. The same who produces for you fire out of the green tree, when behold you kindle therewith your own fires. Is not He who created the heavens and the earth able to create the like thereof? Yea, indeed for He is the creator supreme of skill and knowledge, infinite. Verily, when He intends a thing His command is to be and it will be. So Glory to Him in whose hands is the dominion of all things and to Him will ye all be brought back". The Holy Qur'an says to show the sign of power of God and the creation of the universe "Do they not look at the sky above and see how We have made it and adorned it and there are no flaws in it and the earth – We have spread it out and set thereon mountains standing firm and produced therein every kind of beautiful growth in pairs, to be observed and commemorated by their devote turning to God and We have sent out from the sky rain charged with blessing, and We produce therewith gardens and grain for harvests; and tall and stately palm-trees, with shoots of fruit-stalks, piled one over another; as sustenance for God's servants; and We give new life therewith to land that is dead; thus will be the resurrection...

Were we then weary with the first creation that they should be in confused doubt about the new creation?

WILL

The world goes according to the Will of God and the Holy Qur'an draws our attention to how it was first realised that the Will of God controls everything, such as "And a sign for them is the night: We withdraw therefrom the day and behold they are plunged into darkness; and the sun runs its course for a period determined for it: that is the decree of Him the Exalted in Might. The All-knowing and the moon We have measured for it mansions to traverse till he returns, like the old and withered lower part of a date stalk. It is not permitted to the sun to catch up the moon, nor can the night outstrip the day. Each just swims along in its own orbit according to law. And a sign for them is that We bore their race through the Flood in the loaded Ark; and We have created for them similar vessels on which they may ride. If it were not Our Will We could drown Them. Then would be there no helper to hear their cry, nor could they be delivered.

SIGHT AND HEARING

God sees and hears everything hidden or open. In the Holy Qur'an there are many verses attributing these two qualities of God, such as:

"For God hears and knows (all things)"

"But fear God and know that God sees well what you do"

"God sees well whatever you do".

"God commands you to render back your trusts to those to whom they are due; and when you judge between man and man, that you judge with justice; verily how excellent is the teaching which He gives you, for God is He Who hears and sees all things".

ETERNITY

To God are attributed such things as Eternity regarding the beginning and the end. He was there before everything and He will be there after everything. There is no limit to His beginning and there is no limit to His

continuation. He is the First and the Last. He has neither
the beginning nor the end. We call this in Arabic. *Al Qidan
wa Al Baqa*. It is described in the Holy Qur'an as follows:-

> *"He is the First and the Last, the Evident and the
> Eminent, and He has Knowledge of all things".*

BELIEF IN GOD, HIS ANGELS, HIS PROPHETS, THE REVELATION AND THE LAST DAY

As we have discussed in the first year, it is essential
for Muslims to believe in God and His attributes as we
mentioned in detail before, and also the belief in creation
of the angels, those who were created to carry on the
message for His creatures. The Holy Qur'an describes
them as follows :-

> *"O you who believe, save yourselves and your families
> from the fire whose fuel is men and stones over which
> are appointed angels stern and severe, who finish not
> from executing the commands they receive from God,
> but do precisely what they are commanded".*

BELIEF IN THE PROPHETS

A part of our belief, as Muslims, is to believe that
God sent prophets to many nations. Some of their names
were mentioned in the Holy Qur'an and some were not.
But what is sure according to the Holy Qur'an is that a
prophet was sent to each nation. Our duty as Muslims is
to believe in those whose names are mentioned in the
Holy Qur'an. Prophets must have certain qualities. They
must be free from any illness, come from families of high

standard, and possess many other qualities, such as truthfulness, honesty and courage. God always assists them by miracles in order to convince those to whom they are sent. It is also the duty of Muslims to believe that the Prophet Muhammad was the last prophet and that his message was the comprehensive one. These prophets receive the revelation from God. The revelation carried the teachings of God to mankind. In the Holy Qur'an there are some books of revelation mentioned such as the Bible given to Jesus, the Torah given to Moses, the Zabur given to David and the plates given to Abraham. The Holy Qur'an is the last revelation from God. It contains many indications to the previous nations, prophets and holy books. Belief in what is written in the Holy Qur'an is one of the corner-stones of the belief of Islam.

BELIEF IN THE LAST DAY

Muslims must also believe that after death all of mankind will rise again one day in front of God and He will ask them about their deeds. Those who have faith and have done good deeds will go to Paradise, but those who deny the existence of God and His prophets and have done bad deeds will be questioned by God and subjected to punishment. All of this was taken from the second part of the Hadith which was related before. It says: "When the Angel Gabriel came to the Prophet while he was sitting among his companions in the mosque, and he asked him a question in three parts. The second part was "Tell me about faith". He replied "It means that you should believe in God, His angels and His holy books,

His prophets and the Last Day, and that you should
believe that both decreeing of good and evil are from
God"

PART II

WORSHIP

CHAPTER 2

Worship, *Ibada, Salat*

The Five Daily Prayers have been explained last year, but it will be helpful to give a brief account of them before dealing with other prayers.

1. *Fajr* – morning prayer – It is two *Rakats* and the time starts from when the light of dawn appears in the sky and ends at sunrise.
2. *Zuhr* – noon prayer – four *Rakats*. The time starts from the middle of the day and ends at mid-afternoon.
3. *Asr* – mid-afternoon prayer – It is four *Rakats*. The time starts after the end of the noon prayer and ends at sunset.
4. *Maghrib* – sunset prayer-it is three *Rakats*. The time starts after the sun sets and continues for nearly one and a half hours.
5. *Isha* – night prayer-it is four *Rakats*. The time starts nearly one and a half hours after sunset and continues until the time of dawn.

These are the five daily compulsory prayers and the other prayers, which come occasionally, are as follows :-

> *The Witr Prayer*
> *The Tarawih Prayer*
> *The Prayer in the Time of Fear*
> *The Eid Prayer*
> *The Prayer during Travel*
> *The Prayer at the eclipse of the sun and moon*
> *The Prayer for Rain*
> *The Funeral Prayer*

WITR PRAYER

This is an important Sunnah Prayer performed after the Isha prayer, and it can consist of three Rakats or of one Rakat. Some Muslim Scholars prefer to perform three Rakats together, as we perform the *Maghrib* prayer, and some of them prefer to say two *Rakats* first, separately, and afterwards, ending with *Taslim*, pray the third one alone. There is nothing special to be said in the *Witr* prayer above what we usually say in other prayers. It is Sunnah to perform this prayer in the last part of the night.

According to Hanafi it is *wajeb* and *Qunut* should be said.

TARAWIH PRAYER

Tarawi prayer is said only during the nights of Ramadan, to be performed after *Isha* prayer. The number of *Rakats:* Some scholars say it is eight *Rakats* and some say it is twenty *Rakats*. Either is correct but it is better to perform every two *Rakats* together. One can perform them in the Mosque, or at home.

The Prophet did not pray *Tarawih* in a *Jamah*. He prayed them alone and sometimes in the Mosque and sometimes at home. But at the time of the 2nd Caliph, Omar Ibn Al-Khattab who started to pray them in the Mosque with the *Jamah*; He prayed 20 *Rakats* and people nowadays follow what the 2nd Caliph had done.

PRAYER IN THE TIME OF FEAR

There were times when the Muslim army was facing other armies during the time of war and also in the time of peace. War is something of the nature of life-you cannot stop it-and Muslims in the beginning of Islam received many attacks and they had to answer the attacks of their enemies and defend their land and their religion. This meant that the army had to stay on the frontier for a long time-may be days, may be weeks and may be months or years. The expectation of an attack from the other side was possible at any time. What can the members of the army do during such a time when the time of prayer comes and how can they perform their prayers ? In fact, there is a certain way to offer the prayer during such a time and, at the same time guard the Muslim army and to deal with any attack made by the enemy during the prayer time. There are two ways of offering the prayer, according to the position of the enemy.

If the enemy is not standing in the direction of the *Keblah* and it is the Morning Prayer the *Imam* will stand facing the *Keblah* and the army will be divided into two parts. One part will start praying with the *Imam* while the other part will remain facing the enemy so as to be ready to deal with any sudden attack. The *Imam* prays the first *Rakat* and the part of the army who started to pray with him will follow and complete the prayer. While the *Imam* prays the second *Rakat* the two parts of the army change places, so that those who had been guarding the frontier can join the *Imam* during his second *Raket* and complete their prayers, while the *Imam* waits for them to end the prayer together. This is the arrangement which is made when the prayer has two *Rakats*.

However, when the prayer has four *Rakats*, such as *Zuhr*, *Asr* and *Isha*, the prayer will take another form. The first party will stand with the *Imam* for the first and second *Rakats* and the end their prayer and take over the position on the frontier while the *Imam* is saying the third *Rakat*, waiting for the other party to join him. When the second party joins the *Imam* for the last two *Rakats* they will end the prayer with him. In that case, the *Imam* will have prayed four *Rakats* and each party will have prayed two *Rakats*.

The explanation given above applies when the enemy is not facing in the direction of *Keblah*, but if the enemy is facing in direction of *Keblah*, the *Imam* will start the prayer and when he prostrates himself one party will join him, while the other guards the frontier and Watches the enemy. As the first party finishes the prostration the other party will complete their prostration and will stay with the *Imam* and both will end the prayer with him.

There is another case when the two parties will join the *Imam* at the beginning of the prayer, but one of them will stand facing the enemy while the party will follow the *Imam* until they finish the first *Rakat* and then they will take their place to face the enemy and the other party will join the *Imam* in the prayer, but before joining him they will pray the first *Rakat* on their own and then join the *Imam* and follow him in the second rakat. Then the other party will come again and pray the second *Rakat* while the *Imam* is saying the *Tashahhud* and all of them will end the prayer together.

It is clear from this explanation that prayers during war time is only of two Rakats, except at Sunset, when it is three. This from of the prayer is taken from the verses of the Holy Qur'an, which says:-

"When you, O Apostle, are with them and stand to lead them in prayer, let one party of them stand by in prayer with thee, taking their arms with them. When they finish their prostrations let them take their position in the rear and let the other party come up which has not yet prayed and let them pray with thee, taking all precautions and bearing arms. The unbelievers wish that you were negligent about your arms and your baggage and assault you in a single rush but there is no blame to you if you put away your arms because of the inconvenience of rain or because you are ill, but take other precautions for yourselves. For the unbelievers-God has prepared a humiliating punishment".

This explanation has been given by the Holy Qur'an as is mentioned above, but when the war is over the prayer will have to go back to the regular form. The Holy Qur'an says when you pass congregational prayers celebrate God's praises standing, sitting down or lying on your side, but when you are free from danger pray in the regular way enjoined on believers at stated times.

EID **PRAYER**

Before going into the Eid prayer, we know there are two Eids a year. One is *Id-Al-Fitr*, follows immediately after Ramadan, and the second is *Id-Al-Adha*, which comes at the end of the season of pilgrimage. On the day of the *Eid* there is a special prayer for this particular day. It should be performed by Muslims twenty minutes after sunrise. The time during which this can be done continues until noon. The habit of the Prophet was to have something to eat on *Eid Al Fitr* before going out, and to go to the Mosque by one route and after the prayer to return by another route, so that he could greet as many people as he could.

But how does one perform the prayer? After the opening *Takbir (Takbirat Al-Ihram)* you should say seven *Takbirs*, then recite *Al-Fatiha*, then recite another short chapter from the Quran. It is preferable to read a chapter of *Al-Ala*, again completing the prayer in the usual way. when you start the second *Rakat*, you say five *Takbirs*, then recite the chapter of *Al-Fatiha*, then recite another short chapter from the Quran. It is preferable to recite a chapter of *Al-Ghashia* again completing the prayer in the usual way. Usually the Eid prayer is said in the *jama* gathering and the *Imam* says the prayer out loud. After the Prayer, the *Imam* stands in the front of the Mosque and the people sit in front of him to listen to the sermon. It is like the sermon which is delivered on Friday, but it

contains nine *Takbirs* in the first part and seven *Takbirs* in
the second part. On *Id-Al-Fitr* the *Imam* should encourage
Muslims to give alms for the poor, telling them the
sayings of the Prophet and explaining to them their duty
to pay *Zakat-Al-Fitr* to the poor on that day.

On *Id-Al-Adha* the performance of the prayer is
identical but during the sermon the *Imam* should explain
to the people the significance of the day of Al-Adha and
explain how the Prophet made sacrifice as a reminder of
what the Prophet Abraham did before him, when he
wanted to sacrifice his son, and on *Id-Days*, whether it is
Id-Al-Fitr or *Id-Al-Adh*a, it is *sunna* to say *Takabir* after every
prayer during the three days of *Id-Al-Fitr* until Asr (mid-
afternoon prayer) and to do the same on *Id-Al-Adha*.

PRAYER DURING TRAVEL

These five daily prayers should each be offered at a
certain time when a Muslim is at home or is not traveling.
However, sometimes, it is necessary to be traveling from
place to place or from one country to another: and it may
well be that there are no facilities for preparing oneself
for prayer, or that the timing of the travel will interfere
with the proper performance of prayer.

Islam therefore allows a Muslim, when traveling from
one place to another, to join two prayers together at one
time, such as *Zuhr* and *Asr* the time of *Zuhr* or *Asr*. But
if the Muslim decides to join the two prayers together at
the latter time, he should have the intention during the
time of the first prayer of joining the two prayers later.

The same permission is also given to Muslims to

join the sunset and night prayers whilst traveling. A Muslim has the right to join the two prayers together either at the time of the beginning of the first prayer or at the time of the latter. But there are some conditions which must be fulfilled:-

1. *The traveling must be lengthy -- at least 50 miles.*

2. *It must be traveling for a worthy purpose.*

Also for the purpose of making it simpler for the Muslim to perform his prayer duties, it is permissible to offer *Zuhr* and *Asr* each of two *Rakats* instead of four, and also the night prayer, *Isha*. These are the ordinary cases in which Islam allows us to shorten prayers and join them together. But in some other cases permission is also given to join two prayers together, such as illness or when heavy rain prevents people from getting to the Mosque as usual, or when there is excessive heat. These are sufficient reasons.

The previous permission to join prayers together and to shortenthem has been taken from the verse of the Holy Qur'an which says:-

> "When you travel through the Earth, there is no blame attached to you if you shorten your prayer for fear that the Unbeliever may attack you, for the Unbelievers are born enemies unto You".

According to this verse, it seems that, if there is no fear during the travel, there is no need to shorten the prayer; and this was commented upon by Omar, the second Caliph, who was asked why God gave us permission to shorten and join together prayers. Omar replied that he too had wondered the same thing, and said: "Then I mentioned this to the Prophet (peace be upon him!), and his answer was that this must be considered as one of the charities of God: we have to accept it."

PRAYER AT AN ECLIPSE

When the moon and the sun are in eclipse, there is a special prayer to be offered at that time, as it is stated by the Prophet (peace be upon him). In the Prophet's day's there was no explanation of this phenomenon, but now, in our scientific times, we know when the Moon and the Earth will be nearest each other and when an eclipse may be expected. Therefore, prayer should be made at these times to ask God to save mankind.

But let us examine how it first happened in Islam, and how we should offer prayer. It was the belief of people before Islam that when such an event as an eclipse took place, it was a sign that a great man had died; and when it happened at the time of the Prophet, it fell on the same day as the death of his son, Abraham. People therefore said that it happened because of the death of the Prophet's son. The Prophet knew that this was not the case. Therefore he gathered people together and told them: "The sun and the moon are not eclipsed because of anyone's death or because of his birth, but they are two of God's creatures. So, when either of them is eclipsed, pray until it clears or until God produces something".

But how should the prayer at an eclipse be offered?

The best explanation of how to offer this came from the authority of Ibn Abbass, who said: "The sun was in eclipse at the time of the Prophet, who called for prayer and prayed with the people.

When he started his prayer, he stood for a long time while he recited the chapter of *Al Baqar*. Then he bowed for a long time. Next, he stood again, for a long time but not as long as the previous standing. Then he made another bow shorter than the first. Then he stood. Next, he prostrated himself, as usual. Then he stood up again for a long time, although not as long as before. Then he made another bow, again shorter than before. Then he stood long and bowed and stood and prostrated himself. When he finished his prayer, the eclipse was over. Then he said: "The sun and the moon are two of God's creatures. They are not eclipsed on account of the death or birth of anyone. If you see the eclipse happen, then remember God".

From this explanation, we can see that the prayer for eclipse takes a different form from other prayers in Islam, Each prayer in Islam includes a bow in each *Rakat* includes two long bows and two long standings; and so the prayer for eclipse has two *Rakats*, four long standings, four long bows and four prostrations.

PRAYER FOR RAIN

In many countries they arrange their life according to the amount of rain which falls on their land. The water which comes from the rain will be used for drinking themselves and for watering their land and their animals.

When the rain falls at the right time there is no problem, but sometimes the clouds fail to give the rain at the right time and it is delayed. When this happens, particularly in hot countries, it creates very great trouble for the people and we have heard, during our own time, how much the people of some African countries have suffered from drought. If such a thing happens in a Muslim country Muslims are required to offer prayer for rain.

We are going to explain what happened during the Prophet's time and his direction as to what people should do in such cases.

It happened during the Prophet's time that there was a drought and people were suffering greatly because of it. One Friday, when the Prophet was preaching in the pulpit, somebody came from the desert while he was preaching his sermon and said "O Prophet of God, ask Allah to send us rain, for we suffer much from drought". No plants grow and therefore there is no food for the cattle, and we have no milk or water to drink either for ourselves or our cattle". Then the Prophet started to ask God, while he was still giving his sermon, to send rain to the people, so that they would not suffer. Before he finished his prayer a cloud appeared in the sky, and the rain started to fall and continued until the next Friday. On the next Friday the same man came and requested the Prophet to ask God to stop the rain, because the country was flooded. The Prophet smiled, and prayed to God to make the rain cease, and it happened.

On another occasion, in the ninth year of Hijrah while the Muslim Army was on its way to Tabuk it was summer time, and the heat was severe and they had to pass through a desert, where there was no water, and they suffered much from drought, so much so that they slaughtered their camels and drank the water which was inside the stomachs of the camels. After this had continued for some days Abu Bakr told the Prophet about it and said "Would you please ask God to send them water". The Prophet said "Would you like that? "and Abu Bakr said "Yes, please". Then the Prophet started to pray asking God to send them water and Allah caused a cloud to come over them and the rain fell until they had enough for their camels and themselves.

These two occasions happened but there is a certain type of prayer to be offered when rain is needed, asking God to send the rain. It consists if two *Rakats* and the details are as follows:-

It should be in a gathering and the ruler will lead the prayer. After the opening one should say seven times *"Takbir"* (The magnification of God) and raise his hands each time. Then recite *Al Fatiha*, the opening Chapter of the Qur'an and then recite either the Chapter of *Qaf* or the Chapter of *Al A'La*, then bow as usual, then stand, then prostrating himself twice as usual in the ordinary prayer. At the second prostration the first *Rakat* is ended. Then stand again and say *"Takbir"* five times and then recite either the Chapter of the Moon or the Chapter of *Al Ghashia*. Then make the ordinary bow and standing and prostration. After the prayer the Imam will stand in the pulpit and deliver the sermon like as that of the Eid Day but, during the sermon he would repeat the asking for God's forgiveness.

A'isha, the wife of the Prophet, reported that people complained to the Prophet of God about the lack of rain, so he gave orders for a pulpit to be set up in a place he appointed and gave a certain day on which the people should gather there. He came to the place of prayer on the appointed day and went into the pulpit. Then he declared God's greatness and expressed His praise and said "You have complained of drought in your place and the delay in receiving rain at the usual time and God has ordered you to supplicate Him and has promised to answer your prayer." Then the Prophet said "Praise be to God, the Lord of the Universe, the Beneficient, the Merciful, the Dominion of the Day of Judgment. There is no God but Allah, who does what He wants. O God, there is no God but, Thee the Rich, while we are the poor. Let the rain fall down on us and make what you send to us strength and satisfaction us for a time". Then he raised his hands and kept them raised. Then he came forward to the people, came down from the pulpit and then prayed two *Rakats*. Then Allah caused a cloud to come, which brought thunder and lightening and then rain came down with the permission of God. The place where the prayer was offered was far from the Mosque and when the Prophet reached his Mosque it was flooded and people were going quickly to find some place away from the rain. When the Prophet saw this he smiled and said "I testify that God has power over everything and I am His servant and His messenger".

FUNERAL PRAYER

There is a certain arrangement which has to be carried out when a Muslim dies, and it is best to explain this to you now. When a Muslim dies he should be placed facing Makkah. When death comes the body should be washed with clean water to which some eau de cologne has been added, and the water should be allowed to run over the whole body. The one who washes the body should press the stomach, so that if anything remains it will come out, and afterwards the body should be wrapped in three pieces of white cloth, each one covering the whole body. One piece will suffice if there are no others. After that, the body is buried, lying on the right side, facing Makkah, and the *Janazah* prayer must be performed, before the body is placed in the ground. (This is *Fard Kifiyah*). If only one person is able to perform this it is enough, but it is better for a number of people to perform it. If nobody offers to do it the whole community will be held responsible for that before God. One point I should mention: a woman should only be washed by a woman and a man should only be washed by a man.

HOW TO PERFORM THE PRAYER

The *Janazah* prayer has a different form from the other prayers. It has neither *Ruku* nor *Sujud*. It consists of four *Takbirs*. After the first one the *Fatiha* should be recited, then a second *Takbir* and the blessing on the Prophet should be recited, in the form in which we say it at the end of the prayer. Then a third *Takbir* is said. After the third *Takbir* we have to say some kind of invocation (*Dua;*)

then a fourth *Takbir* and *Salam* as the sign of the ending of the prayer. The performance of Salam is: *"As-Salamu Alaikum Wa Rahmat Allah Wa Barakatuh"*. This means: "Peace be upon you and the blessing of God and His mercy". This means that the prayer has ended.

ZAKAT

Zakat is one of the five pillars of Islam, its aim is to meet the social need of the Muslim Society and to improve the economic position in Islam.

The word *Zakat* means purification, blessing and increasing. It is a kind of protection to the wealth of those who are rich. When a Muslim pays his *Zakat* he is protecting his money from unexpected disaster, for the Prophet said : "Protect your property by giving Zakat and help your relatives to recover from their illness by giving charity.

Zakat is an obligatory payment, like a tax, and the English translation is "Poor Dues". It could be called a divine tax for it has been prescribed by God in the Holy Qur'an and in the sayings of the Prophet. The holy Qur'an says in many places "Keep up regular prayer and give Zakat", and of the sayings of the Prophet when Mu'adh was sent to Yeman was "You will come to folk who are people of the Book, so invite them to testify that there is no god but God and that Muhammad is God's messenger. If they obey that, tell them that God has made it obligatory for them to pray five times every twenty four hours. If they obey that, tell them that God has made it obligatory upon them for *Sadaqa* to be taken from the rich and handed over to the poor. If they obey that, do not take the best part of their property, and have regard to the claim of him who is wronged, for there is no veil between it and God".

There are many kinds of *Zakat*: *Zakat Alfitr* which is an obligatory payment by a Muslim slave or freeman, male or female, young and old, and it should be made before the *Id* prayer. It is usually given from the food of the majority-wheat or grain or barley. The cost of this could be given instead and it is preferable, in a country like England, for it to be done by giving money. Now-a-days, one must pay 50p for each member of the family, including the servant (if there is a servant) and one's parents, if one is responsible for them. Ibn Abbas said "At the end of Ramadan bring forth the *sadaqa* as a *sa'* of dried dates or barley, or half a sa' of wheat, payable by every freeman and slave[1], male or female, young or old". Ibn Abbas said that God's messenger prescribed the Zakat relating to the breaking of the fast as a purification from empty and obscene talk and as food for the poor.

Other kinds of *Zakat* are *zakat Almal*, meaning money *Zakat*, whether it is gold silver; *Zakat Altijara*, meaning Trade *Zakat*; *Zakat Alanam* meaning Cattle *Zakat*, involving camels, cows or sheep; *Zakat Alzuru Waalthimar*, meaning cereals and fruits. These last two are of one kind. For *zakat* to be compulsory there must be two conditions; first, that it must reach the *Nisab* and secondly (see below) that it must have been owned by the payer for one complete year.

1. The Money *Zakat*

When anyone has a sum of money, whether it be gold or silver and the amount of this money reaches a certain sum called *Nisab* and he has owned this money for one year then 2.5% of it must be paid for the *Zakat*.

The *Nisab* of silver is two hundred Dirham and the *Nisab* of gold is twenty Dinar. If this money is more than is needed for himself and his family and he keeps it in the bank, or in a safe or uses it to be increased by lawful means, then it will be subject for *Zakat* and 2.5% must be paid for every year. If the amount of money is increased, then the payment must be increased also. For instance, if someone had $100 in hand he would pay for *Zakat* payment for the second year would be $5 and so on.

2. Trade *Zakat*

Zakat is compulsory on trade and other businesses like companies or firms if the two conditions are fulfilled, first that it reaches *Nisab* and secondly that it has remained in the possession of the owner for a complete year. Then the payment would be 2.5%. Suppose someone starts his trade or business with a capital of say $100,000, at the end of the first year of trading he must find out the total value of his trade, including his profit, and if it comes to $200,000 at the end of the first year then he must put aside 2.5% from the $200,000 and pay this for *Zakat*; and he must do the same every year. This is Trade *Zakat*.

3. Cereal and Fruit *Zakat*

There is a certain system employed in paying cereals and fruit *Zakat*. The cereals which are subject to *zakat* are those used for food, such as wheat, barley, corn and beans, and the fruits subject to *Zakat* could be dried fruits, such as dates, grapes and figs. When harvest time comes for the cereals and fruit the farmer or the landlord will reckon up his harvest and, if his land is watered only by the rain or water coming from river without the use of machinery, then one-tenth of the complete value of the harvest must be paid as *Zakat*. If, however, the land was watered by machinery or by the labour of man, then the payment will be one-half of the one-tenth. This method of calculation could also be used for fruits.

4. Cattle *Zakat*

Some African and Arab countries have a lot of cattle, such as camels, cows and sheep, but in this country people generally own, or are employed in, factories shops and businesses of other kinds. Islam prescribes *Zakat* on this kind of property also, if it reaches a certain value, which is known as Nisab.

This kind of *Zakat* is obligatory if three conditions are fulfilled:-

1. The value of *Nisab* must be different in one kind of *Zakat* from another kind.
2. The property must have stayed in the possession of the owner for one year.
3. For cattle, they must have a free pasture in which

they can get their food, without labour or food being bought for them.

With regard to the Zakat for camels, if you own five camels and they are in your possession for one year and they have free food from a public pasture then you must give, at the end of the first year, a young lamb, less than one year old.

> *If the number becomes ten, then two young lambs are due.*
>
> *If the number becomes fifteen, three young lambs are due.*
>
> *If the number becomes twenty, four young lambs are due.*
>
> *If the number becomes twenty five, a young she-camel more than one year old is due.*
>
> *If the number becomes thirty six, one young she-camel more than two years old is due.*
>
> *If the number becomes forty six, a she-camel more than three years old is due.*
>
> *If the number is sixty-one, a she-camel more than four years old is due.*
>
> *If the number becomes seventy six, two she-camels more than two years old are due.*
>
> *If the number is between ninety one and one hundred and twenty, then two she-camels more than three years old are due.*

If the number of camels exceed one hundred and

twenty there is a special way of calculating Zakat, which is as follows:-

One she-camel, more than two years old, is due on every forty camels and one she-camel more than three years old on every fifty and so on.

Concerning the zakat on sheep which are pasturing, when they number from forty to a hundred and twenty a sheep is to be given.

On over a hundred and twenty, up to two hundred, two sheep are to be given.

If they exceed three hundred a sheep is to be given for every hundred.

If man's pasturing animals are less than forty no zakat is due on them unless the owner wishes.

An old sheep, one with a defect in the eye, or a male goat is not to be brought forth as zakat unless the collector is willing.

Those which are in separate flocks are not to be brought together and those which are in one flock are not to be separated from fear of zakat.

Regarding what belongs to two partners, they can make claims for restitution from one another with equity.

Regarding Cows, if the number of cows reaches thirty then one young cow, one year old will be taken as Zakat.

If the number reaches forty then one cow, two years old will be taken as Zakat.

If the number reaches sixty, then two cows of one year old will be taken as Zakat.

If the number reaches seventy then two will be taken as Zakat, one of them two years old and the other only one year old.

If the number reaches eight, then two of two years old will be taken.

On ninety, three of one year old will be taken.

On one hundred, one of two years and two of one year will be taken.

On one hundred and ten two of two years and one of one year will be taken.

On one hundred and twenty three of two years old will be taken.

Islam has prescribed *Zakat* for all kinds of property for the benefit of needy people. It is not always paid in money but, in some cases, in cattle, cereals and fruits as in Africa and similar countries. But in England and other European countries, trade and business are the most common way of paying *Zakat* and money is used for this purpose. The aim of collecting *Zakat* is to serve members of society and to meet their needs and help them to overcome the difficulties they are facing. Some people are in difficulty because they have not the ability to work, some because they meet with disaster of some kind and some because they are old and need help. *Zakat* in Islam will be the source of security for members of society from any hardship. Those who have the right to receive money from *Zakat* are mentioned in the Holy Qur'an in the following verse:-

Alms are for the poor and the needy and those
employed to administer the (funds); for those whose
hearts have been (recently) reconciled (to truth), for
those in bondage and in debt; in the cause of God; and
for the wayfarer. (Thus it is) ordered by God and God
is full of knowledge and wisdom.

In case there is nobody who is in need of Zakat it
will be collected and the head of the community will
spend it for the benefit of the whole, using it, for example,
for the building of schools, hospitals, mosques and other
similar things.

FASTING FOR THE MONTH OF *RAMADAN* IN ISLAM

The fasting of Ramadan is one of the five pillars of
Islam. This is because the Prophet (peace be upon him)
said Islam is upheld by five Pillars; first to bear witness
that there is no God but Allah alone and that Muhammad
is His Messenger. Second, to pray regularly. Third, to
pay *Zakat* i.e., divine tax for poor due. Fourth, to fast
during the month of *Ramadan*. Fifth, to visit the House of
God in Makkah once in a lifetime, of those who are able
to do the journey.

Fasting for the month of *Ramadan* was prescribed
during the second year of the *Hijara*. Fasting was an
ancient form of worship prescribed by God from the
beginning of time. The aim of ordering people to fast is
that they should learn how to be patient, to have good
morals, to purify their hearts, noble their character and to
practice the gentle way of dealing with people. One
should feel the sufferings of hunger and thirst in order to

be quick to help those who are suffering when seeing them. One must always learn to feel the fear of God and His Mercy.

Fasting in Islam has been prescribed by the Qur'an and the saying of the Prophet. The Qur'an says "O you who believe, fasting is prescribed to you as it was prescribed to those before you, that you may learn self-restraint". This is for fasting in general, but the following verse gives the reason for fasting during the month of *Ramadan*. It says:- "*Ramadan* is the month in which was sent down the Qur'an as a guide to mankind, also clear (signs)for guidance and judgment between right and wrong. So every one of you who is present at his home during the month of Ramadan should spend it in fasting". Besides this, there are many sayings of the Prophet (peace be upon him) which emphasise the time of fasting for the month of Ramadan.

We will take only one of the Prophet's sayings, because it will be enough for us that this saying has been related by al-Bukhari, on the authority of Anas Ibn-Malik, one of the Companions of the Prophet and his servant. He said "While we were sitting with the Prophet (peace be upon him) in the Mosque, a man came along riding his camel. After he had ordered the camel to kneel and had tied it up outside the Mosque, he asked "Which one of you is Muhammad?" "It is that fair man who is reclining there", someone answered. The man came up to the Prophet and said "Oh son of Abdul Al Muttalib". So the Prophet said " I am ready to answer you", and the man replied: "I am going to ask you some harsh questions so please do not be offended regarding them".

The Prophet said "Ask whatsoever you like". The man asked "In the name of your Lord and the Lord of those who came before you is it really God who has sent you to all mankind?" The Prophet answered: "Yes, by Allah He has". The man again spoke: "I ask you in the name of God, did God order you to pray five times every twenty four hours?" the Prophet answered: "Yes, by Allah". Then the man said "I ask you in the name of God, did God really order you to fast this month every year? "The Prophet answered yes, by "Allah". Again the man asked a question: "By the Name of Allah is it really God who orders you to take "Zakat" the divine tax from the rich people and distribute it among poor people?" the Prophet answered: "Yes, by Allah".

Then the man said "I believe in what you have brought us from God and I am the messenger of my people". He then mentioned the name of his tribe. From these teachings, and from the Qur'an also, it is clear that the fast of *Ramadan* is a duty for both the male and female, once they have reached the age of responsibility and have the ability to fast.

THE HONOUR OF *RAMADAN*

The month of Ramadan is an honourable month. It is the season of good, during which the mercy of God is sent down to His servants, the fates of good action will be opened and the opportunity of forgiveness and of pleasing God the Almighty are available. Many of the sayings of the Prophet (peace be upon him) gives statements regarding the honour of the month. Some of them are as follows:-

Al Nisai related that the Prophet (peace be upon him) said "The month of Ramadan has come to you, it is a blessed month. God the Almighty makes the fasting obligatory upon you. The gates of heaven will be opened during it, the doors of hell will be closed, the chiefs of Satan will be chained. One of the nights of that month is better that a thousand months, and it is the night of Power (*Lailet al Qadr*). Whosoever does not gain its honour will lose all kinds of good".

And al-Bukhari related, on the authority of Abu Huraira, that the Prophet said "When Ramadan comes, the gates of paradise will be opened, the doors of fire will be closed and Satan will be chained".

Those who fast during the month of Ramadan for the sake of God and hoping for His mercy, have been promised forgiveness by God, according to the saying of the Prophet (peace be upon him): "Whoever fasts the month of Ramadan and prays during the night for his belief in God and for the sake of God, his previous sins will be forgiven; and whosoever spends the Night of Power (*Lailet al Qadr*) in worship for the sake of God, his previous sins will be forgiven".

The most comprehensive tradition of the Prophet regarding the honour of Ramadan is the one related by the authority of Salman al –Farisi. He told how God's messenger said, in a sermon which he delivered on the last day of Sha'ban, " A great month, a blessed month, a month containing a night which is better than a thousand months has approached you people. God has appointed the observance of fasting during it as an obligatory duty, and the passing of its night in prayer as a voluntary practice. If someone draws nearer God during it with some good act, he will be like one who fulfils an obligatory duty in another month. It is the month of endurance, and the reward of endurance is paradise. It is the month of sharing with others, and a month in which the believer's provision is increased. If someone gives one who has been fasting something with which to break his fast it will provide forgiveness of his sins and save him from hell, and he will have a reward equal to his, without the reward being diminished in any respect".

Some people remarked to God's messenger that they did not all have the means to give one who had been fasting something with which to break his fast. And he replied; 'God gives milks mixed with water, or a date, or a drink of water with which to break his fast; and anyone who gives a full meal to one who has been fasting will be given a drink from my supply of water by God and will not thirst till he enters paradise. It is a month whose beginning is mercy, whose middle is forgiveness, and whose end is freedom from hell. If anyone makes things easy for his slave during it, God will forgive him and free him from hell".

THE REWARD OF FASTING

The reward of the accepted fast is Paradise. God the Almighty gives great reward for fasting as much, or more, than we can realise. This is because fasting is secret between man and his Lord, therefore it is the only one among the aspects of worship that has been attributed to

God. It has come down to us in the traditions of the prophet (peace be upon him) that he said "Any kind of good act in done by the children of Adam will be rewarded from ten times to seven hundred times and it may be more, according to the will of God". God said "Accept fasting for it is an attribute of me and I will reward it, because one who fasts is giving up his desires and his food for my sake". The one who fasts has two occasions of happiness; one when he breaks his fast and the other when he meets his Lord. The smell of the mouth of one who fasts is better than perfume in the sight of God.

Another tradition is that God said "All the kinds of good works done by the children of Adam are for him, except fasting which is for me, so I will pay the reward for it. Fasting is a protection. When one of you is fasting he should not speak bad words, he should not raise his voice. If someone insults him, or fights him, he should remind himself that he is fasting by saying "I an fasting, I swear by God, who has Muhammad's soul in His hand, that the smell of the mouth of the one who fasts is better than perfume in the sight of God".

HOW TO OBSERVE THE BEGINNING OF THE MONTH

The beginning of the month of Ramadan, and every month in Islam will be decided after seeing the new moon. When any Muslim sees the moon it means that the month has started, for the Prophet (peace be upon him) said: "Fast when you see the moon and stop fasting when you see the next new moon. If, because of cloud or fog, you cannot see the moon then complete the month of sha'ban in thirty days".

The month in Islam can be thirty days or it can be twenty nine days, according to the appearance of the moon. It is not necessary for everyone to see the moon himself, but it is quite enough to know that the moon has been sighted through accepted sources. This is because the Prophet (peace be upon him) ordered his companions to fast when he was informed by someone that the moon had been sighted and ordered them to stop fasting when he was informed that the new moon had been seen. There are a number of traditions attributed to the Prophet (peace be upon him) dealing with this matter, such as that of Ibn Umar, one of the Prophet's companions (may God be pleased with him and his father) said "Some others and myself were looking out for the moon, when I informed the Prophet that I had seen it, and he started to fast and ordered the people to fast".

Ibn 'Abbas (may God be pleased with him and his father) related that a bedouin came to the Prophet and said " I have seen the moon". Then the prophet asked him "Do you bear witness that there is no God but Allah?" the man said "Yes, I do". The Prophet asked again, saying "Do you bear witness that Muhammad is the messenger of Allah?" "Yes, I do", the man replied. Then the Prophet said to Bilal, "O Bilal, tell the people to fast to-morrow". One can conclude from these two Hadiths that if only one man sees the moon of Ramadan it will be enough for the month to start, and it is enough for his *Shahada* (witness) to be accepted if he says "I am Muslim", because this was the only thing that the Prophet asked.

THE CHARACTERISTICS OF FASTING

As we know, fasting occupies a high position in Islam; its reward is great. To realize how great it is remember what the Prophet said regarding it: "Fasting is sacred between man and his Lord". Knowing God promised to give a reward for it shows how deep its influence is on the souls of mankind, and how immediate is its effect in directing man towards good deeds and letting good will to prevail in his heart. Therefore there are many sayings of the prophet (peace be upon him) to encourage Muslims to keep this worship free from any fault which may prevent its good result coming to those who fast.

Those faults are:- Hypocrisy, which will corrupt sincerity; bad words, which lose man the respect of others; quarrels between people, which leads to spite and helps destroy the rights of mankind.

Many sayings of the Prophet warn us from committing these mistakes and call upon Muslims, to adopt good moral characteristics which will help them draw nearer to God. This will come naturally after their hearts have been cleansed and souls purified. There is one such saying: "Whoever does not stop speaking falsehood and acting accordingly, God has no need for him to give up his food or drink." Other sayings warn people about using bad words. For instance, when anyone starts fasting he must stop swearing and control any urge to harm others, and he should not revenge himself upon anyone who tries to harm him, always remind himself that he is fasting.

Fasting is a protection from evil, but if one allows oneself to speak ill against others or to tell a lie the protection is destroyed and one faces the attacks without any help. The Prophet said "Fasting is a protection against hell, it is exactly like a protective coat of armour which you would wear when you prepare to go fighting". The fast will be an active protection unless man stops its action by speaking lies or talking ill of others. Above all, man must be sincere, because when sincerity directs you, you will do your best to please God alone and to gain spiritual progress without caring about the suffering from hunger or thirst. To keep yourself thus you must remember that it is only for the sake of God. If you try to show people that you are a man of morality and devotion then you will spoil your worship, because you will have allowed hypocrisy to ruin your heart. In this case you will not get any reward from your fasting but the suffering from hunger and thirst, as the Prophet said "There are many people who fast but they have no reward to gain from their fasting except the suffering from hunger and thirst, and there are many people who spend the night praying and they gain no reward from their prayers except to be awake all night".

THE HOURS OF FASTING

The time of fasting is from, dawn to sunset and it is recommended by Islamic teachings that you break your fast immediately after sunset; it is also recommended that you break it with a fresh date or a dry one or any other fruit. If there are no dates or fruit break your fast with some water. Then pray, and after prayer have your meal. It is also recommended that you break your fast with a certain prayer which the Prophet used to repeat. All of these teachings have been taken from the traditions of the Prophet and we will now give the origins of them.

First, regarding the time of fasting, a man named Sahl ibn S'ad, one of the companions of the Prophet, said "When God revealed the following verse of the Qur'an 'Eat and drink until you distinguish the white light from the darkness' some people hearing this verse wanted to fast. They tied a white and black string on their legs and hands and continue eating until they could see both of them. But this is not the meaning of the verse, which alludes to the light of the dawn appearing through the darkness. Therefore these words were revealed. "Let them eat and drink until they can distinguish the light from the darkness "from the time of the dawn". Then those people recognized that the meaning of this saying "the white and black string" represented the day and the night, and from this they understood that to start fasting was the time of the dawn. The time of ending the fasting has been taken from the tradition as related on the authority of 'Umar, that the Prophet said "When night comes from this direction," (and he pointed with his hand towards the West) "and the sun sets, then the time of breaking the fast has started".

It is impossible for those who live in the North or South pole areas, and have no regular day or night to follow the day and night concerning prayer and fasting, or to arrange their fasting and prayer according to day and night. Because sometimes the sun is visible for six months and then it disappears for six months. Muslim scholars have two opinions about what those who live in such areas should do. Some scholars say they could arrange their day and night according to the country nearest to them which has regular day and night. But this would be very difficult to put into practice, because in some countries in the North, the light continues for twenty or more hours during the summer and it is not possible for people to fast for this length of time. There is difficulty also regarding the prayer. I believe it will be accepted, from a religious point of view, for us to use the permission to join the 'Isha' and the Maghreb prayer together, in order to be able to pray in the morning at the right time.

The other group of scholars say that the people who live in the North Pole area can arrange their time according to the time of Makkah, where mostly the day and the night are equal. The people can, therefore, fast for twelve hours and arrange their time for prayer by Makkah time also, whether the sun is visible or not; this would be the most acceptable way of arranging prayer and fasting because it is logical and easy to put into practice. So it is allowed for Muslims who live in these areas to measure their times according to Makkah time. This is because Makkah is nearly on the equator and therefore it has nearly equal day and night. But, above all, because it was there that the revelation to the Prophet Muhammad started, and there is set up the House of

God to which we direct our faces when we pray, and we go there for pilgrimage.

SOME MUSLIM TRADITIONS DURING RAMADAN

The instruction which has led us to break fast immediately after sunset has been taken from the saying of the Prophet, "People will be in good condition as long as they have the habit of having early breakfast". The companions of the Prophet followed this instruction strictly. And it has been related that a man named Abu 'Atiya said " I went with Masruq to see 'Aisha (the wife of the Prophet)and said 'Oh Mother of all believers, we are coming to ask you about two companions of the Prophet (peace be upon him) one of whom had the habit of having an immediate breakfast and immediate prayer after sunset and the other used to delay breakfast and the prayer. Would you please tell us which one of them was following the way of the Prophet?" She asked them about the one who ate and prayed immediately after sunset and they told her his name was AbdAllah Ibn Mas'ud. Then she said 'Thus the Prophet (peace be upon him) used to do".

The habit of breaking the fast with fresh or dry dates or other fruit is taken from what has been said regarding the way of the Prophet, as follows"- "The Prophet used to break his fast with some dates before he went to prayer. If he did not find dates then he had some waster to break his fast with. It was the habit of the Prophet to end his fast with the following prayer "O God, for Your sake I

have fasted and have broken my fast with sustenance
you gave to me. The thirst has gone and the reward from
God is coning with His Will".

AbdAllah Ibn 'Amr related how the Prophet said that
when someone is fasting and prays to God his prayers
will not go unanswered. It was the habit of AbdAllah
when he broke his fast to say "O God, I ask You through
Your mercy, which is so wide that it contains everything,
to forgive my sin".

Many sayings of the Prophet give promise of great
reward to those who give food for others to break their
fast with. And also to those who encourage people who
fast to pray for the one who offers food to them. This is
because such behaviour will strengthen human
relationships between members of society. And doing
good things helps to make people good, as well as
creating a feeling of unity among members of society,
unity in their aims, their faith and in their belief in God
Almighty. But, above all, it will help people to be of
noble character. Therefore, the Prophet (peace be upon
him) said "Whoever offers food to those who are fasting
will gain an equal reward to their reward without
decreasing their reward".

It was the habit of the Prophet to pray for those who
offered food to the people who were fasting. Once he
broke his fast in the house of one of his companions
named Sa'd Ibn Mu"adh (may God bless him) and after
having the meal the prophet said this prayer: "Your food
has been eaten by the righteous, so may the angels bless
you and may your name be mentioned in the presence of
God.

TRAWIH PRAYER

One of the characteristics of the month of Ramadan is to have a special prayer during the night, which we call the *Tarawih* Prayer. We have been directed by the Prophet (peace be upon him) to offer this prayer during the nights of that month, for he said "Whoever prays during the month of *Ramadan* for the sake of belief receives forgiveness from God. God will for give him his previous sins". The majority of Muslim people practise twenty *rak'ats* every night and gather in the mosques to do this. But some Muslim scholars say the number of *rak'ats* should be only eight, because the Prophet (peace be upon him) did not pray more than eight.

SUHUR

It is one of the customs of Muslims to have a meal during the night near to the time of dawn, in order to sustain them to carry on the fast during the day. This meal, named *Suhur*, is especially for Muslims. It was not allowed for the previous nations (who came before the Muslims) when they were fasting to have any meal during the night after the meal at sunset. This was also the case for Muslims at the beginning of Islam, but then God permitted them to have food during the night, up to the time of dawn. The Prophet (peace be upon him) named this "The Blessed Meal". It is also recommended that his meal should be taken as near as possible to the time of dawn.

All these recommendations regarding *Suhur* have been derived from the saying of the Prophet: "Have your meal of *Suhur* because it is a blessing" and also one of his companions related that he went to the Prophet while having his meal of *Suhur* and the Prophet said "It is a blessing that has been given to you by God. Do not miss it". This *Suhur* is considered as something special for the Muslim nation because the Prophet said "The difference between our fasting and the fasting of the people of the Book is that we have the meal of *Suhur*". It is also considered as a sustenant because the Prophet said "Sustain yourself to continue fasting during the day by having the meal of *Suhur*.

UPON WHOM FASTING IS COMPULSORY

Fasting is compulsory upon those Muslims who reach the age of responsibility, who are sane, and those who remain in their homes and traveling and all those who are in good health. Those who have the ability to fast, as does the woman who is free from her monthly period and also has lost the placenta after giving birth to a child. If these conditions are fulfilled then fasting is compulsory for all these people. But the people who are not Muslims are not asked to fast, neither is the insane person subject to fasting nor the young boy or girl. If a young boy or girl fasts this will be acceptable, but it will not be acceptable if a non-Muslim or an insane person fasts, because they have not the basis of teaching in their minds.

Regarding boys and girls, their fathers have the right to ask them of fast from time to time, in order that they can get used to doing this and when he or she reaches the age of responsibility it will be easy for them to carry, on condition that they have the ability to fast. This is because the tradition had been related, on the authority of 'Alrubaiy, the daughter of Mu'awwith, who said "The messenger of God (peace be upon him) sent a message on the morning of the day of 'Ashura (the tenth day of the month of Muharram) to the village of al-Ansar saying 'Whoever starts his day fasting he should complete the fast, and he who did not start the day fasting must fast for the rest of the day'. She also said "We used to fast the day after that and let our children fast and we used to go to the mosque. When the children cried because they were hungry we used to give them a doll made of wool in order to quieten them until it was time to break the fast".

THOSE WHO ARE EXEMPTED FROM FASTING

Those who are exempted from fasting are old men and women, the sick man or woman who has an incurable sickness, those who have heavy physical work to do so that they con not fast, soldiers who are in battle areas and travelers. All these people are exempted from fasting during Ramadan. Some of them will be exempted for the rest of their lives; and such people as the old men and women, the incurably ill and those doing continuously physical work, who are unable to fast, should instead pay for enough food for one person each day. This is called *"fidya"*. Pregnant woman and women who are breast feeding their babies are also exempted, if their fasting would affect them or their babies, but they have to pay *fidya*. Some of the companions of the Prophet exempted these people altogether from fasting. But those who are traveling or have a temporary illness, or do heavy work, and are not able to keep the fast always have to fast during the number of days that they did not fast during Ramadan, and this they must do before the next Ramadan.

Sometimes fasting is forbidden. If the fast would create harm to anybody or would cause death, then one must break the fast, even if one is at home or in good health. The reason why fasting, in these cases, is forbidden is the fear of the resulting harm that might be caused to the one who fast, for the Holy Qur'an says:- "Do not put yourself in a position that would create harm for you" and the Prophet says "there is no harm in Islam". The main source from which we take these ideas regarding fasting is the saying of God: "Do not kill yourself, verily God is merciful to you", and also His saying "God does not make any difficulty for you regarding your religion". It has been related that once, when the Prophet was joining the army during Ramadan he broke his fast and ordered the soldiers not to fast.

It is obvious, when Islam asks those who are exempted from fasting to pay Fidya, if they are able to do so, that those who are unable to do this will certainly also be exempted from this payment.

There are some cases which exist now-a-days, such as pilots of aeroplanes, train drivers and those who work as car drivers all of whom have responsibility for the lives of their passengers, who have the right to be exempted from fasting because, if they fast, it could affect their control of the machines or might mean that they were not fully conscious of their actions. This people are exempted from fasting for the benefit of the lives of their passengers, but they have to pay fidya.

All that we have said, regarding those who are exempted from fasting of some reason or other, has been derived from the saying of God in the Holy Qur'an "The month of Ramadan is the month in which the Holy Qur'an was revealed as a guidance for and judgment between right and wrong. So every one of you who lives to see this month shall fast throughout it, but those who are ill, or on a journey, during Ramadan must fast the number of days corresponding to those they have lost during the fast. This is because God does not want to make difficulties for you. He wants to make it easy so that you complete the number of days of fasting and so you magnify God for His guidance of you. So that you are able to do your duty to your Lord".

Those who are asked to fast a number of days instead of those days on which they should have fasted during the month of *Ramadan* have to do it before the coming of the following *Ramadan*. They could offer it on one day a week, two days a week or could do it for the stated number of days continuously. There is no compulsory way of doing this.

Some people, during *Ramadan*, eat or drink at a time which they sincerely thought was before dawn, but after having eaten and drunk, they realized that the dawn had started. If this happens unintentionally there is no sin, but they have to keep away from food and drink all that day and after Ramadan they have to fast one extra day, instead of the one they missed. It is the same for those who eat and drink thinking that the time of fasting has finished, because they think the sun has set, but later on realise that the sun had not set when they had eaten. But both of them, whether they had eaten at the beginning of the day or at the end of the day, are free from sin because of their good will. This happened at least once in the lifetime of the Prophet, as related on the authority of Asma', who said "We broke our fast during the life of the Prophet on day when it was cloudy, but we were surprised afterwards to find that the sun was there, so we were ordered to repeat one day of fasting".

Sometimes during the day one sincerely forgets the fast and eats or drinks something. If this happens there is no sin and there is no duty to make up the day but, one's fast must continue. If someone feels sick, but does nothing to make himself sick his fasting will not be spoiled, but if he puts his fingers down his throat to encourage sickness, then his fast is ruined and he must fast another day instead.

Sometimes a man is sleeping during the day and dreams that his wife is sleeping with him, this will not ruin his fast, but if he does such an action in reality, not in the dream, while he is aware of it during the month of *Ramadan* it ruins his fast and he will be under an obligation to make a *Kaffara* (expiation). First of all, he has committed a great sin during the month of Ramadan and secondly he must make a *Kaffara* as follows, in three parts:-

First to give freedom to a slave. If he is not able to do this, then he must fast continuously for two months and if he is not able to do this either, he must feed sixty poor persons. This is derived from what happened during the time of the Prophet, when a man came to him and said "O Prophet of God, I have gone astray" and the Prophet asked him "How have you gone astray? "the man said "I have slept with my wife during the month of *Ramadan*". The Prophet asked "Could you free a slave?" and the man said "No". Then the Prophet asked "Could you feed sixty poor people?" and yet again the man said "No". Then while they were sitting there a big sack of dates was brought to the Prophet, so the Prophet gave it to the man and said "Give it as a charity". Then the man said "No one in this area has a greater need that mine" and then the Prophet smiled and said "Give it to your family to eat".

If anybody breaks his fast during Ramandan without any reason then he is subject to make a *Kaffara* as is set out above.

To break your fast during Ramadan without reason is a great sin, and the one who allows himself to commit such a sin will lose all precious reward. For the Prophet said "Whosoever breaks the fast of *Ramadan* during the day without reason of without illness, he will not be able to compensate for this, even if he spent all his life fasting".

Whosoever has broken the fast during Ramadan for a recognized reason and has to make it up by fasting for a corresponding number of days after *Ramadan*, but dies before he has completed his fast, then his heir will be responsible for the number of days lost and must fast instead of the person who dies. For the Prophet said "Whoever dies while he is obliged to fast, then his heir will fast instead of him". Ibn 'Abbas related that man came to the Prophet (peace be upon him) and said "O Messenger of God, my mother has died and she has to fast for a month, is it permitted for me to do it on her behalf?" And the Prophet said "Yes, for and obligation to God is worthy to be done".

THE HABIT OF THE PROPHET DURING THE LAST TEN DAYS OF RAMADAN

It was the habit of the Prophet during the last ten nights of Ramadan to increase his worship. He used to spend the whole night in worship and encouraged his family to do the same, according to their ability, and he kept away from his wives. 'Aisha, the wife of the Prophet, said "When the last ten days of Ramadan started the Prophet kept away from his wives and spent the whole night worshipping and encouraging his family to do the same.

Lailat al Qadr, or The Night of Power, is one of the nights in the last ten nights of Ramadan and this night is a blessed night. God made it honoured and better than a thousand months. This is because the Holy Qur'an was begun to be revealed on this night and it is said in the Holy Qur'and "In the name of God, most gracious, most merciful, We have revealed this (message) in the Night of Power, and what will explain to thee what the Night of Power is ? The Night of Power is better than a thousand months. Therein comes down the angels and the spirits descend by the leave of their Lord upon command. Peace it is until the rising of the dawn".

Whoever spends this blessed night in worship, his previous sins will be forgiven, for the Prophet (peace be upon him) said "Whoever fasts the month of Ramadan for the belief in, and sake of God, his previous sins will be forgiven and whoever spends the Night of Power (*Lailat al Qadr*) praying for belief and for the sake of God, his previous sins will be forgiven".

A large number of the traditions of the Prophet encourage the Muslim to believe that the Night of Power is one of the last seven nights of the month. But some traditions make others think that it is one of the last ten nights of the month. Other traditions again, give us to believe that it is one of the odd numbered nights of the last ten nights.

DAYS WHEN IT IS FORBIDDEN TO FAST

It is forbidden to fast on the Day of *al-Fitr*, the Day al *Adha* and the three days of *al-Tashriq*, that follow the Day of *al-Adha*. This is because the Prophet (peace be upon him) prohibited fasting on the Day of *al-Fitr* and the day of *al- Adha* and he said "Regarding the days of *al-Tashriq*, they are days of feasting and remembering God the Almighty".

Ibn Azhar said "I attended the day of *Id al-Adha* with 'Umar ibn Alkhattab (may God be pleased with him) and I heard him saying "These two days (by which he meant the day of *al-Fitr* and the day of *al-Adha*) are days on which the Prophet has forbidden fasting. They are the days which follow your fasting and the days on which you eat from your sacrifice".

Besides these days there are a number of days on which it is not encouraged in Islam that you should fast. One of these days Friday, for the Prophet said "Do not fast on Friday, unless you join it to the days before or the days after it". Neither is it encouraged to fast on Saturday, except when it comes during the fast of Ramadan the month of fasting.

HAJJ (PILGRIMAGE)

Pilgrimage to Makkah is one of the five Pillars of Islam. It is obligatory for every able Muslim to visit Makkah once in his life-time for pilgrimage because the Holy Qur'an says:-

> "Pilgrimage is a duty man owes to God. Those who can offer the journey ..."

and the Prophet said:-

> "Islam is built upon five Pillars. First, there is no other God but Allah and Muhammad is His messenger. Second to keep the five daily prayers. Third, to give Zakat, the divine tax. Fourth to fast during the month of Ramadan and fifth to perform the Pilgrimage to the House of God in Makkah, for those who are able to offer the journey".

Hajj, in Islam, means visiting the sacred Mosque in Makkah during certain dates in the Muslim year, which are called "the months of Hajj". These months are

Shawwal, Dhu al Qada, and Dhu al Hijja. The pilgrimage to Makkah can only be accepted at these times and the condition of performing Hajj cannot be accepted before these months, for the Holy Qur'an says:-

"The Hajj is performed in certain months".

There is another kind of visit to Makkah which is called *Umra*. It is compulsory once in a lifetime for those who are able to perform the journey, but the difference between *Umra* and Hajj is that *Umra* can be offered any time during the year. It could be joined with Hajj, or it could be performed alone. The best time to perform *Umra* is during the month of Ramadan, for the Prophet said *"Umra* during the month of Ramadan is equal to Hajj".

The reward of Hajj and *Umra* is a great reward in the sight of God, for the Prophet (peace be upon him) said:-

"To offer Umra is to abolish the sin committed before and if you offer two Umras, whatever sin you committed between them will be abolished or forgiven and the reward for an accepted Hajj is Paradise".

Condition for Hajj to be compulsory

Hajj is compulsory on all Muslims reaching the age of responsibility, sound in mind, a freeman and able to offer the journey. The condition is that he should be financially and physically able and should have sufficient financial resources for himself and his family during his journey and until his return. The way of going to Makkah must be safe from known dangers. Without these conditions being fulfilled it is not compulsory.

The Rites of Pilgrimage

To perform the Hajj there are a number of rites which must be fulfilled:

The first thing to do is to enter *Iharam* which means the Sacred State, and then the one who is performing Hajj must carry out the following conditions:-

When the pilgrim comes near to the places in which he should put on *Iharm*, he should cut his moustache and hair and nails, have a bath or ablution, put some perfume on his body and then put on the dress of *Iharam*. Then he should pray two *Rakats*, and have the intention of performing Hajj or *Umrah*, or both of them together. This is one of the most essential things of the pilgrimage and should not be dispensed with. Once the pilgrim has done these he has started on the sacred state which we call *Iharam* and then he should start the *Talbiah* with a loud voice, particularly when he climbs to a high place, or descends to a low place, or meets a group of people, or a single person, and towards the end of the night, and at the end of each prayer.

The one who is in the sacred state (*al-Muhrim*) must avoid the following things:-

1. To go to his wife.
2. To have a dispute with his friends.
3. To have a useless argument about something.
4. To marry, or arrange the marriage of another.
5. To wear sewn clothes and to wear shoes which cover the ankles.
6. To cover his head, or to touch perfume, or to shave or cut his hair.

7. To cut toe or finger nails.
8. To hunt, or eat meat obtained by hunting.
9. To cut the trees or grass of al-Haram (the sacred place).

When he enters Makkah it is preferable for the pilgrim to enter it from the upper side, after having had a bath, if this is possible, at a well which is found before you enter Makkah, called *Dhu-Twua*. Then he should go to the Sacred Mosque, al-Kabah, enter it from *Bab-al-Salam* (the door of peace). While he is calling upon God and remembering Him he must bear in mind the sacred state of the Mosque, showing his humility before God, and saying the *Talbiah*. As he sees the Kabah, he should go directly to al *Hajar al-Aswad*, the black stone, kissing it without making a sound, or touching it with his hand and then kissing his hand. If it is not possible for him to do this, he could make the gesture the stone, say the prayer and start the *Tawaf*. The *Tawaf* will be made seven times. It is preferable to touch other side of the Kabah, which is named al *Rukn al Yamani* (which means the Yamani corner) and to kiss the stone, if it is possible, at each Tawaf.

After *Tawaf*, the pilgrim should then come to Al *Multazm* (which is the name of the door of al-Kabah) and he should there ask God to bless him with goodness in this world and the next. He should then go to a place named *Maqam* Abraham (the Station of Abraham), reciting the saying of God "Takye, the station of Abraham for a place of prayer" and pray there two *Rakats*. Then he should go to the Well of Zamzam and drink from its water and come out of the mosque by the door of al Safa, reciting this verse from the Qur'an:

> "Behold al safa and al Marwah are among the symbols of God. So if those who visit the House in the season or at other times should compass them round, it is no sin in them".

Then he should climb the hill of al safa, direct his face towards al Kabah, praying to God, repeating the prayer we have mentioned before. Then he should go down from the hill and walk from al Safa to al Marawah, using a certain path on the walk. Whilst walking he should keep remembering God and calling to Him. When he reaches the other side to the Hill of al Marwah, he should climb the hill, direct his face towards al Kabah, calling on God and remembering Him. This should be repeated seven times.

If the one who is in the sacred state wants only to perform Umra, after the seven times he should shave or cut his hair and end the sacred state, and his Umra is completed. But if he is in the state of Hajj, or Hajj and Umra together, he should keep his sacred state and go on the eighth day of Dhu al-Hijjah to a place outside Makkah called Mina and spend the night there. After sunrise he should go to the Mountain of Arafat, and stop at the Mosque there called Namirah Mosque, and have a bath if it is possible and pray Zuhr and Asr, together with the Imam, both of them at the time of Zuhr, if it is possible. If not, then the pilgrim prays alone, standing on Arafat, starting immediately after noon. And the pilgrim should stand at the place called al sakharat, or near to it, because the Prophet stood there. Standing on Arafat is the most important part of the pilgrimage, for the Prophet said: "Pilgrimage is Arafat". It is not permitted to climb up to the Mountain of Mercy. While he is standing he should direct his face towards al Kabah and say the *Duaa*, and remember God. The pilgrim stays there until sunset and, after sunset he should go to the place called Al Muzdalifa. There he will pray *al-Maghrib* and *al-Isha* at the time of Isha and spend the night there. After the dawn of the following day he should stand at a place which is named al-Mashar al-Haram, and remember God, up to sunrise, then go to collect his stones. Then he should go back to Mina.

After sunrise on the tenth day of Dhual-Hijjah, the pilgrim will throw seven stones at a place called Jamrat al'Aqabah. Then offer his sacrifice, if it is possible, then have a shave or cut his hair, and in doing that he will be able to do the things which have been forbidden to him whilst he was in the sacred state, except to have relations with his wife. Then he should go to Makkah performing *Tawaf al-Ifadah* which is the most important one, and he should do it seven times as explained before. After this Tawaf, the condition of the sacred state will be ended completely, and it will be permitted to have relations with wife. Then the pilgrim should go to Mina and spend the night there. Immediately after noon on the following day (11ᵗʰ Dhual-Hijjah) he should throw down the stones in three places, starting with the place called Jamrah, which is next to Mina. Then throw seven stones, in another place called al-Jamrah al_Wusta (the middle one) and stay after throwing the stones, remembering God and calling Him. Then he should go to the third place, which is named Jamrat al-Akabah, throwing the other seven stones, and then go without staying there. He should repeat this throwing in the three places on the 12th and 13th days of Dhual-Hijjah, then he should go to Makkah to prepare himself for returning to his home.

After he decides to go back, he should bid farewell to the House of God, with the last *Tawaf* named *Tawaf al-wada*, and by doing this all the deeds of pilgrimage will be finished, but it is preferable for those who perform the pilgrimage to go to visit Madinah the town of the Prophet and greet his Mosque and his grave and to spend some time there. His visit could take place before performing Hajj, or after it.

PART III

LIFE

CHAPTER 3

Aspects from the Life of the Prophet

INTRODUCTION

The life of the Prophet Muhammad (peace be upon him) is the most excellent example to follow both for Muslims and for non-Muslims. His teaching, his character, his behaviour and his guidance are all very fine roles for people to carry out the living of peaceful, happy and healthy lives. Whenever you read about his life you will find him emphasizing that people should be tolerant that they should co-operate with each other, love each other and help one another for the benefit of all mankind. His teaching made it clear from the beginning that all mankind are equal and the equality among people is the basis for their living together, in spite of their differences in colour, race or tongue for these differences are caused because of difference of the weather, their way of life and so on, but they all come from one origin. They are the children of one father. It is Adam and Adam was created from dust. We can realise the importance of these principles if we bear in mind that at the time of the Prophet Muhammad two-thirds of mankind were slaves and one third were the masters and there was no good reason for slavery to prevail over the majority of mankind at that time. This system of life was followed strictly by all nations at this time and the tribal attitude was dominating the life of mankind. Very many of the verses of the Holy Quran and the Sayings of the Prophet tried to make it clear that all mankind are equal and also his own practice in his society gave an example for people to follow. Equal care has been given to the freedom of man and his right to think, to work and to express his ideas in an equal way with others. The rights of women are carefully considered because of the way woman were treated before Islam and were considered as something that a man could inherit from his father like other property.

It is hoped that we shall deal with these matters in other places, but when we speak of 'Aspects from the Life of the Prophet' we have to give a brief account of his life for the student to understand, although he had it last year, as it is so very important that it should be clear in his mind.

The Prophet Muhammad was born in Makkah, the central religious and commercial city in Arabia. The House of God is there, al-Kabah, which was built by the Prophet Abraham and his son Ishmael thousands of years before the Prophet Muhammad was born.

The Prophet Muhammad was born in the last third of the Sixth Century of Jesus. Some Muslim scholars say

that it was on the 20th April, 571. The Prophet Muhammad
was descended from the Prophet Abraham. His family
occupied a high position among the natives of Makkah
and also among the whole of Arabia because of their
relation to the House of God, al-Kabah. His father died
before he was born in a dramatic event and his mother
died when he was six years old. His grandfather, Abd-al-
Muttalib looked after him and Abd-al-Muttalib was the
chief of all Makkah and had inherited this office from his
family. His grandfather died when the Prophet was eight
years old and then he was looked after by his uncle, Abu
Taleb, who was the oldest of his uncles. Both his
grandfather and his uncle took very great care of him.
When he was twelve years old he went with his uncle to
Syria and there something happened which drew the
attention of people towards Muhammad. The caravan of
Makkan people reached the border of the Syrian desert
and were met by a monk, whose name was Buhaira. He
invited them to eat and they were surprised to receive
this invitation, because they passed him every year and
saw him in the same place, but he had never before invited
them to eat. They accepted the invitation and when the
food was ready the old men in the caravan went and
started to have their food. It was noticed that the monk
was looking very carefully amongst them as though he
was looking for something important. It has been related
that he had noticed a cloud following the caravan when
it came near to him and when they sat down to eat he
missed the cloud, but noticed that it stood above their
camp. Then he asked 'Have you left anybody in your

camp?' They answered 'Yes', a young boy. We left him there to look after our things'. Then the monk said 'Please call him', and one of the people said 'I swear by God it is not right for us to leave the son of Abd Allah', and he went and brought him. while they were eating the monk watched Muhammad carefully, but after they had eaten he came nearer and spoke to him saying 'O boy I ask you by Allat and Al-Uzza (the names of two of the idols the people of Makkah worshipped). The Prophet said 'Don't ask me by these two idols, I never hate anything as I hate them'. The monk said 'I ask you by the name of God to answer my questions' and Muhammad answered what he wanted. After that the monk asked 'Who is the father of this boy?' His uncle said 'I am'. The monk said 'No, his father should not be alive', so Abu Taleb said 'I am his uncle'. Then the monk said 'Be careful and look after him, because if the Jews come to know of him, they will kill him'. It has been said by historians that the monk knew from his own divine books according to the signs he found; that Muhammad would be the coming Prophet.

When the Prophet returned to Makkah he used to work as a shepherd to help his uncle, who had a large number of children. The people of Makkah were amazed at his behaviour, character and sense of responsibility. As we know, Makkah was a commercial centre and many of the rich people of Makkah sent their trade to Syria and Yemen, with people to look after it and to sell their goods there and to return with goods from Syria and Yemen to be sold in Makkah. One of these rich people in Makkah was Khadija. She was a rich woman from one of the highest families in Makkah and she sent her trade to Syria and Yemen. When she heard of the honesty and character of Muhammad she offered to let him look after her trade to Syria. This offer he accepted and went to Syria. The caravan set out to go to Syria under the care of Muhammad. He was accompanied by a slave named Maisara, who was astonished by the noble character of Muhammad and the excellent treatment he received from him. In his company he felt that they were not slave and master, but that Muhammad was dealing with him as brother to brother. The caravan went to Syria and came back with great profit for Khadija, who was amazed by the honesty of Muhammad and what Maisara told her about him. Khadija was a rich woman from a high family of Quraish, but she felt that it would be good for her to be married to Muhammad, although she was forty years old and he was only twenty five. Muhammad was poor but his family held the highest place of honour among the Makkan people and the marriage would have to be arranged in a very delicate and tactful way. Khadija talked to one of her friends, explaining her wish to be married to Muhammad and her friend went to Muhammad asking him why he did not get married and the following discussion took place:

Woman   : O Muhammad! Why don't you get
                   married ?

Muhammad : I have no means to enable me to
                   get married.

Woman   : But if you were asked to get
                   married to one who is beautiful,

	rich and honoured would you accept ?
Muhammad :	But how can I find such a person?
Woman :	Don't worry, I will arrange it.

and she told him about Khadija. When, after the matter was discussed with Khadija it was known there was no objection and that the arrangement was agreeable to both sides the Prophet got married to Khadija. He was only twenty-five-years-old and she was forty years old, but they were very happy and Khadija lived with the Prophet for twenty eight years, during which time he never married another wife and during which time she helped him with her many kindnesses and assistance. When he faced difficulties outside she was the one who met him at home and made it easy for him. They had seven children most of whom died during the lifetime to the Prophet. The People of Makkah were astonished by the character, the behaviour and honesty of the Prophet Muhammad and they called him 'Alsadeq Alamin', meaning 'the trustworthy'. When the Prophet was thirty-five-years-old an event took place in Makkah which created division among the Makkan people that they nearly fought each other, but were saved from this grave event because of the wisdom of Muhammad. This event was when they decided to rebuild al-Kabah, the Sacred House in Makkah. When they reached the stage where they had to replace the Black Stone, Al-Hajar al-Aswad, each tribe wanted to have the honour of doing this and the arguments increased until they were ready to fight each other because of this.

Some of their leaders saw how grave the situation was and put before the people a suggestion which was accepted. The suggestion was that they would accept the judgment of the first person who came from a certain direction. After listening to this suggestion and agreeing to it the people all looked towards that direction to see who would be the first person to come and judge the situation.

When they saw Muhammad coming they all cried out with happiness and said 'This is *Alamin'* (the trustworthy) and, with a sigh of relief they put the matter in his hands. When they told him the reason for the division he asked them to choose four representatives, one from each tribe, and to get a piece of sheeting in which he put the Stone and asked the four representatives to carry the piece of sheeting in which the stone had been placed and when they reached the spot where the stone should be replaced he took the stone in his two hands and replaced in its proper place. This is the first recorded public action of Muhammad and it save the people of Makkah from bloodshed through his wisdom.

It was the habit of the Prophet Muhammad to spend one month every year in a cave on the top of a mountain near Makkah and there he meditated and thought about the right religion and asked God's guidance to show him the religion of Abraham, because he refused to accept the belief of the people of Makkah, who worshipped idols. This continued for a number of years. When he was forty years of age the Archangel Gabriel came to him and informed him, in a very convincing manner, that he was a Prophet from God. The details of this will be mentioned in another place. He received the first revelation after becoming a Prophet which said:-

'Read in the name of thy Lord who created, created man from a clot. Read and thy Lord is most beneficial. He taught by pen. Taught man what he knew not'. When the Prophet received this revelation from God and when he became sure then he continued to call people to accept the new religion, which was based on the oneness of God, worshipping only Allah and giving up the worship of idols, which many men of intellect never accepted. His call went through many stages, for the first three years it was secret and after that it was an open call. He stayed in Makkah for thirteen years, calling the people to the religion of Islam, during which time further revelation came to him and he also faced many difficulties from the leaders of the Quraish who realised the danger of the new religion, which threatened their position in Society. The struggle continued for thirteen years, during which many events took place and then the Prophet emigrated to Madinah where he established a Muslim society and a Muslim state. He stayed there for ten years, during which time all the Arabian peninsular became a Muslim land as they accepted the call of Islam and during these years many events took place which we will deal with later on. Also during these ten years the revelation came continuously. When the Prophet reached the age of sixty three years he died.

This is a brief life of the Prophet and in the following pages we will look at some aspects of this great life for the purpose of study and as an example.

THE DAY OF PEACE

When the Prophet was thirty-five years old, the people of Makkah wanted to rebuild Al-Kabah, because it had been damaged by the floods which covered the valley of Makkah at that time. The tribes of Makkah co-operated with each other to rebuild Al-Kabah, because it was an honour for them, and all the Arab tribes. All the Arab people respected the Makkans and regarded them as the people who looked after the House of God.

When they started building they came to the place where they had to replace *Al-Hajar al Aswad*, the Black Stone. From this moment the arguments started. Who would have the honour of putting the stone in its place? Each tribe wanted to have this honour. They started arguing, and this almost led to a fight. Some of them called for a fight, and a blood bath threatened Makkah. The wise leaders of the tribes recognised this as an extremely dangerous situation and they wondered what they could do to prevent this tragedy. One leader suggested that they should accept the judgment of the first man to enter the place. This suggestion was readily accepted, because nobody wanted this threat to continue; they were afraid of the consequences, as they might well all be killed. They all stood with their eyes facing towards the way which led to Al-Kabah. Then they saw the Prophet, Muhammad coming towards them. At that time Muhammad had not claimed to be a Prophet but he was the most highly respected man in Makkah and renowned for his honesty and trustworthiness. For this reason they used to call him *'Al-Sadiq Al-Amin'* – 'The Trustworthy, the Truthful', and when they saw his coming all of them cried with one voice :

'Al-Sadiq Al-Amin!' in a tone of appreciation. And they all felt happy and at peace in their minds and they felt sure no harms would now befall any of them, and that whatever Muhammad's decision, it would be accepted by all. When they explained the problem he requested them to bring a piece of cloth and he chose four men, one from each tribe. He then placed the stone on the cloth and asked each of the four men to take one corner. The four men then shared the carrying of the stone until they came near to the wall, and the Prophet then took the stone in his hands and put it in its place in the wall.By making this decision he was able to prevent the 'blood-bath' and peace prevailed in Makkah. This, too, was the first day that the people realised the outstanding wisdom of Muhammad and he came to be regarded as the most revered person in Makkah. We could call this day 'The Day of Peace'.

THE BEGINNING OF THE REVELATION

It was the practice of the Prophet Muhammad, before he reached the age of forty, to go to the cave on the Mount of Hira near Makkah every year to spend one month there to worship according to the religion of Abraham, and to seek for the truth, because the people of Makkah were worshipping idols, and this Muhammad could not accept. Once, at the age of forty, while he was there, he heard a voice coming from the sky, calling to him:

'O Muhammad'

He raised his head, looking towards the direction of the voice and he saw the Angel Gabriel in a place between the sky and the ground, saying to him:

'O Muhammad, you are the Prophet of God, and I am the Angel Gabriel'.

This was a shock for Muhammad, and he was amazed. He turned his face away but wherever he turned the voice came to him and he saw the Angel. He could not understand how such a thing could have happened to him and he left the cave and returned quickly to Makkah. But on the way the Angel again appeared to him and the voice of the Angel filled his ears. He was afraid and when he reached his house his wife knew he was worried and he asked her to bring plenty of blankets as he was so cold. Perspiration flowed from his face. When he had become calm and his wife was beside him, he wondered what had happened to him. His wife asked him to explain what had happened as she wanted to remove his worry from his mind.

When he told her, she told him not to worry, and she reminded him that Allah will never disgrace those who help the weak and give money to the poor and spend their lives helping others, as Muhammad had always done. Then he slept.

The Prophet's wife had an uncle called Waraqa Ibn Nawfal. He was an old man and he was one of those who rejected idolatry and was looking for an ideal religion. He had read the Old and the New Testament and followed Christianity. He therefore had a knowledge of prophethood and revelation. From his knowledge he had come to know the religious men of the 'People of the Book', and knew from them that they were expecting the Prophet to come. When he heard what Muhammad's wife told him he knew that Muhammad was the Prophet for whom they had been waiting. Khadija (the wife of the Prophet) went back to her home and asked her uncle to come to them. When he came and the Prophet got up, Waraqa said :-

'O my brother's son, tell me what happened'.

The Prophet told him, and Waraqa said:

'By Allah, you are the Prophet for whom we have been waiting. I hope I shall live until your people drive you out'.

The Prophet asked him:

'Will they drive me out ?'

and Waraqa explained that no-one had ever told his people such things without being driven out. Waraqa promised that if he lived he would do everything he could to help Muhammad.

Once more, Muhammad was in the cave and the Angel came to him and said:

'O Muhammad, you are the Messenger of God and I am the Angel Gabriel'.

Then he embraced him strongly and said:

'Read'.

The Prophet answered :

'I cannot read'.

Then the Angel embraced him again, strongly and said:

'Read'.

The Prophet answered:

'But I am unable to read'.

The Angel embraced him for the third time, more strongly and said:

'Read, in the name of your Lord who created, created man from a clot. Read, and your Lord is generous. He taught by the pen, taught man what he knew not'.

And then the Angel left the Prophet. Muhammad said:

'When he left me I felt as though these words were ringing in my ears'.

And the Angel did not appear to him again for three months.

When he came he revealed to him these verses :

'In the name of God the most gracious, most merciful, O you are wrapped up (in a mantle), arise and deliver your warning and magnify your Lord. Keep your garments free from stain and all abomination shun.

Nor expect, in giving, any Increase (or yourself) but for your Lord's sake be patient and constant'.

And then the Prophet started to call his people to Islam, and the revelation continued after this for twenty-three years, until the Prophet departed this life.

THE DAY OF THE BEGINNING OF THE CALL TO ISLAM

About three years after the Prophet received the first revelation, he was told :

'Warn your close relatives'.

He started to speak to his close friends and his own family. Khadija, his wife, was the first woman to accept Islam, and Abu Bakr the first man. Ali ibn abi Talib, his cousin was the first boy to accept Islam, and Zaid was the first servant to accept Islam. The number started to increase slowly through the personal contact of the Prophet and his close friend, Abu Bakr, but when he received the verse mentioned it was a sign to inform the whole people of Makkah of his cause.

The Prophet climbed a hill there called Al-Safa and started to call out:

'O people of Makkah!'

in a loud voice. They were sitting around Al-Kabah. When they heard his voice they came and gathered round him. He said:

'What would you say if I informed you that there is an army coming to attack you from the other side of the mountains?'

They answered :

'We never knew you to tell lies'.

Then he said:

'I am the manifest Warner, and I am the Prophet of
God to you, and therefore I call you to worship God
alone and not to worship idols'.

It was the first time that the Prophet had made a public announcement of his call, but the people were astonished at the information he gave them, because he had never told a lie, and yet what he asked them was extraordinary. One of his uncles, Abu Lahab got annoyed and spoke to him harshly.

From that time onward, the Prophet started to call people to accept Islam, openly, while at the same time, the people of Quraish started to inflict harm upon him; to insult him and his followers. But this made no difference to him; he continued his call and did not give any attention to the harm he suffered from the people until he emigrated to Madinah, thirteen years after this call.

THE NIGHT OF *AL ISRA* AND *AL-M'RAJ* —THE NIGHT JOURNEY

This event took place nearly three years before Hijrah, and this event is mentioned in the Holy Qur'an. There is a chapter in the Holy Qur'an called Al-Isra. In the beginning of this chapter

Allah says :

'Glory be to Allah
who took his Servant by night
from the invoilable place of worship
to the distant place of worship,
the neighbourhood where of We have

blessed, that We might show
him of Our tokens! Lo! He, only
He is the Hearer, the Seer'.

This is about the journey from Makkah to Jerusalem, and the other journey, from Jerusalem to Heaven. It is mentioned in detail in the Hadith of the Prophet, and some verses of the Holy Qur'an in Surat *al-Najm* refer to this event.

But we have to know why this event took place at this particular time in the life of the Prophet, and what was the significance of it, and exactly what happened during that night. It is related that during the space of one year the Prophet lost his uncle, Abu Talib, who used to protect him from the aggression of the people of Makkah, and also his wife, Khadija, who was a good wife to him, and who used to smooth for him the various difficulties he had to face from people outside the house.

The loss of those two persons in one year caused a lot of sorrow for the Prophet (peace be unto him) and he called this year the year of sorrow. After the death of Abu Talib the people of Quraish harrassed the Prophet more and more, and when he went home he did not find anyone to make it easy for him as Khadija used to do. It was a hard time for the Prophet, and it seemed there was no helper or protector in Makkah. Therefore he decided to go to the town of *Al-Taif*, in which the tribe of Thaqif lived, to call them to Islam, hoping that he would find a helper among them. He started the journey from Makkah to *Al-taif* with his servant, Zaid, and the Prophet kept his journey secret, because he didn't know if the people of

Al-Taif would accept his call or not. When he arrived in *Al-Taif* he began by meeting the heads of this tribe, discussing with them the matter of belief, and inviting them to the religion of Islam. But unfortunately their response was not good, and he had to bear the hardship of receiving their refusal. He asked them to keep his discussion with them a secret in order to keep the people of Makkah from knowing about this failure in *Al-Taif*.

But they would not agree to this, and their words to him were impolite. One man swore by Allah that if the Prophet spoke the truth, then he was their superior and should not speak to them, because discussion between them would be unsuitable. But if, on the other hand, the Prophet were a liar, then he was the inferior of the tribesmen, and it was not suitable for the tribesmen to keep the company of such an inferior!

When the Prophet (peace be upon him) began to leave the town, the people ordered their slaves and naughty children to line the street on either side of his way and to stone him as he walked, until the Prophet's blood flowed and covered his heels. His servant, Zaid, tried to protect him, but was unable to do so. After the Prophet left the town he was in a most unhappy state and sat down under the shade of some trees.

These trees were on the boundary of a vineyard which belonged to two men from Quraish, whose names were Otbah and Shaibah, son of Rabia. These two saw what happened to the Prophet and felt pity for him, and sent a slave of theirs to him with a bunch of grapes. When the Prophet started to eat he said, 'Bismillah ir Rahman ir

Rahim', ('in the name of God, the Merciful, the Compassionate'). The slave was astonished to hear these words, and said:

'Sir, this is a custom not used by the people of this region'.

The Prophet asked him,

'Which country do you come from?'

The man answered.

'I come from Ninawa'.

The Prophet said,

It is the home town of the righteous man, Younos ibn Matta'.

'How do you know Younos?' the man said.

'He is my brother,' said the Prophet. 'He was a Prophet, and I am a Prophet, also'.

Then the man knelt down and kissed the hands of the Prophet. His masters were most surprised to see him behaving in this way. When they questioned him about his conversation with the Prophet, and heard his answer, they warned him not to be affected by the ways of Muhammad.

Then the Prophet raised his hand, praying to God:

'O my Lord! You are my God, and the God of those who are weak, to whom You leave me, to any enemy, giving him control of my affairs; to a foreigner. I ask You, by the Light of Your Face, by which the darkness becomes shinning and by which the whole earth and the heavens stand in order to give me Your help; so long as I know you are not angry with me, I don't care what people do against me'.

After this journey, it was clear there was no help at all from anyone on earth for the Prophet. When he came near to Makkah the news of the failure of his journey had got there before him, and he couldn't enter Makkah without first sending a message to a man called Al Mutim ibn Adyi, asking him to be his protector, as was the custom of the Arab tribes at that time.

It was in this situation that the journey from Makkah to Jerusalem and from Jerusalem to heaven took place, to give spiritual aid to the Prophet, and to assure him that Allah was with him always, even if there was no one to help him from the creation; and at the same time, through this journey he saw many signs to show him the power of God, to give him more aid: as the Holy Qur'an says:

'To show him from among our signs'.

This journey took place during part of one night, and was over before dawn broke. On the next day, when the Prophet informed the people of Makkah about this journey they became enraged and they discussed the Prophet Muhammad, calling him a liar, and they tried to use the strangeness of this event as proof to persuade people to give up the religion. They even tried to influence Abu Bakr (may Allah bless him) with this.

'Do you know what your friend has said?' they asked.

'What did he say?' said Abu Bakr.

*'He claims that he went to Jerusalem during the night
and returned before dawn', they said' 'A journey of
one month each way! How can this be done in a few
hours of the night?'*

'If he said so then he is telling the truth'. The people
of Makkah were astonished.

'Do you believe him, then?' they asked.

'Why not?' Abu Bakr answered, 'I would believe more
than that about him. I believe that the revelation came
from heaven'.

On this journey, when the Prophet was taken up to
heaven he received the compulsory prayer, which
Muslims say five time a day. There are many details about
this journey which are most interesting for a Muslim to
know. There is no need to discuss them now, but if anyone
wants to know about them, let him go to the original
source.

THE DAY OF HIJRAH (EMIGRATION FROM MAKKAH)

This is a very important day in the history of Islam.
The Prophet spent thirteen years in Makkah calling its
people to Islam, using every means he had to help them
accept his call. But for their part, they used every means
to stop him from continuing his call; they hurt him and
they persecuted his followers. They even killed some of
them. They wanted to kill him, too, but they did not try
as they were afraid of his family. But when they could
find no other way to stop him, they had a meeting in a

house in Makkah ('Dar Al-Nadwa'-'House of Serious Discussions') to discuss a way to stop Muhammad from calling people to his religion. During the discussion one of them suggested putting him in prison and leaving him to die, without food or water. The others did not agree with this, arguing that some of his followers would help him to escape or he might persuade the guards to let him go free, as his influence on the people was so profound. Another proposal was that they should drive him out of their country and let him do what he liked elsewhere. But the members of the meeting rejected this idea, also, saying that his words influenced people so greatly that he would soon find other tribes to accept his call and would establish a strong army with thousands of soldiers and everyone would join him. Then the third suggestion was made. They would choose one young man from each tribe in Makkah and each of them would have a sharp sword. They would be ordered to go to Muhammad and all of them would share in his killing. His family would be given the ransom for his life, and would not be able to fight every tribe represented by the assassinators. This suggestion was accepted. They quickly started to put this plan into action and chose the young men who would take part in the plot and the arrangements were made for a certain time and date.

Before this time the Prophet had advised most of his companions to emigrate to Madinah. His friend, Abu Bakr did not go, as the Prophet asked him to stay behind. Perhaps he could find another companion and leave together. When the decision to kill the Prophet was made by the people of Makkah, the Prophet was warned of it through a revelation from God. God ordered him to leave Makkah and go to Madinah on the night they planned to kill him. The Prophet started to prepare for this journey and he went to Abu Bakr one day at noon and informed him what they were do to. He instructed him to make arrangements for the journey and to find someone who had experience of the desert. The day before the night of the departure the Prophet called his cousin, Ali Ibn Abu Talib and asked him to get ready to sleep in his (Muhammad's) house that night in place of the Prophet. He also instructed him to return to the people many things which were in his house. The people put all their trust in Muhammad, and for this reason anyone who had something very precious and wanted to keep it in a safe place would ask the Prophet to take care of it. The Prophet wanted to stand by his duty and return all these things and so had to choose a member of his own family to do this. That night the Prophet went to his bed as usual and during the night these young men came and took their places, standing outside his front door, their hands placed on their swords. They were ready to kill him as soon as he came out; they knew his regular habit of leaving his house late at night to go to Al-Kabah to pray until dawn. It is related that when the Prophet wanted to leave the house God cause then men to feel so tired that they went to sleep while standing in their positions and he came out without their being aware, reciting these verses:

Ya-Sin.
(Of the Signs of God).

By the Qur'an, Full of Wisdom,
The Word is proved true
Against the greater part of them:

Thou art indeed One of the apostles On a Straight Way.
For they do not believe. We have put yokes
Round their necks Right up to their chins,

It is a Revelation Sent down by (Him),
So that their heads are
Forced up (and they cannot see).

The Exalted in Might, Most Merciful,
And we have put A bar in front of them

In order that thou mayest And a bar behind them, Whose
fathers had received No admonition, and who Therefore
remain heedless
Admonish a people And further, We have Covered
them up, so that They cannot see.

And after he had left they woke up and they noticed
the time had passed and thought he had not yet come
out of his house, as he usually did. They saw someone
sleeping in the bed. They decided to wait until daybreak
as they didn't know what had happened. When the sun
rose they saw that the person asleep in the bed was not
Muhammad and they were filled with rage and went
around looking for him everywhere, realising that their
plot had failed. Then they started to search outside

Makkah, offering a reward of one hundred camels to anyone who could find the Prophet, alive or dead.

Let us follow the path the Prophet took when he left the house. He went to his friend, Abu Bakr, who was waiting for him. When he reached his house, Abu Bakr made arrangements with his family and his workmen, and he and the Prophet left together. They went to the cave outside Makkah on the way to Madinah. This cave was called the Cave of Thawr. When they reached this cave the Prophet told his friend they would spend some time in this cave. They went in and stayed there for three days. Abu Bakr asked a shepherd there to graze his sheep around the cave during the day and to come and stay there during the night to inform him of the news from the people of Makkah. This shepherd let his sheep move around the cave until they had removed the footprints of the Prophet and his companion and during the night, he gave them milk and food and informed them of what the people of Makkah were saying about them. During their stay in the cave the people of Makkah came to the mouth of the cave, looking for them. The companion told the Prophet: 'O Prophet, if one of them looked at his feet, he would see us!' But the Prophet answered:

> 'Don't worry, Abu Bakr, no harm will come to those whom God is with'. It is related that there was a spider's web at the mouth of the cave and that a bird came and put two of her eggs there. When the people of Makkah came to the cave and saw the web and the eggs they did not look inside the cave, as someone remarked: 'This was here before Muhammad was born!'

When the people of Makkah left, the Prophet and his companion stayed for three more days and then went on their way. The man who was to be their guide came with three camels, one for himself, one for the Prophet and one for Abu Bakr and he led them out into the desert, using ways which were not known to others.

On their way to Madinah something extraordinary happened. One whose name was Suraka Ibn Malik heard about the reward of one hundred camels and when someone told him that three man had been seen in the desert he knew it must have been the Prophet and his friends. He immediately ordered his horse to be ready and followed them. When he approached them his horse's forelegs sank into the sand and when he tried to lift the horse up he couldn't until the Prophet had gone far ahead. Then Suraka called:-

'O Muhammad, ask God to free my horse and I shall not follow you'.

But when his horse got up the 100 camels made him forget his promise. He started again to follow them, but again, when he approached, the horse's hooves began to sink in the sand. Suraka called again to the Prophet, promising not to follow him, but again he did and the same thing happened for the third time. And Suraka fell from the back of his horse. He swore before the Prophet that this time he really would not follow the Prophet who informed him that when the Emperor of Persia had fallen under Muslim rule Suraka would be given the Emperor's gold cuff links. It is related that this happened in the time of the 2nd Caliph. He remembered the promise

of the Prophet and gave the cuff-links to Suraka. And the
Prophet continued on his way to Madinah. On their way
they felt hungry and thirsty. They passed a tent in the
desert, with a Bedouin woman there. They asked her if
she had something for them to drink. She apologised to
them as she had nothing at all, apart from a very weak,
old goat and this didn't even give milk. When the Prophet
touched the udder, however, it gave plenty of milk and
they drank as much as they wished, leaving a lot for the
woman and her husband. After they had left the woman
was astonished to find that the goat after that continued
to give a plentiful supply of milk! When her husband
came home she told him of the visit of the Prophet and
they always remembered this Blessed day when this
Blessed man whom she didn't know came to her tent.
News of the Prophet reached the people of Yathrib, and
spread through the town, and he was expected there
before his arrival. They wanted to be the first to see him,
and each day they waited for him, and when he didn't
appear, they returned home at midday. One day, they
had returned home at midday, thinking the Prophet
would not arrive, when a Jewish man who had climbed
a date tree saw the Prophet and his companion coming.
He called to the people of Yathrib, telling them 'Your
good fortune has arrived'. This was feast day among the
people of Yathrib, when they saw the Prophet with them.
Everyone wanted to have the Prophet as his guest. As the
Prophet passed by, everyone asked him to honour them
by being their guest: the Prophet told them 'Let the camel
pass and it will stop in a certain place, as she has been

ordered to do'. The camel stopped when it reached the house of Abu Aiyub.

From the day the Prophet settled in Madinah and because of the importance of that day it is regarded as the beginning of the history of Islam.

THE DAY OF *ADHAN* (CALL FOR PRAYER)

After the Prophet had emigrated to Madinah he started to teach his people how to perform the prayer. The problem arose how to announce the time of each prayer. The Prophet discussed this matter with his companions to think of a way that his followers would have of knowing that a congregation was about to assemble. Some of his companions suggested having a big fire lit in a high place, so that people might know that the time had started, but this idea was rejected as it was felt it might be confused with the worshipping of fire, whereas Muslims worship God alone. Another suggestion was that they use a horn as Jewish people did, or ring a bell, as Christians did. Both these ideas were rejected as they wished not to copy other religions, but to have something distinctive for the Islamic religion. No decision was taken at that time but they all went away with the purpose of considering the matter, trying to think of something original and acceptable. One of the companions in particular thought very deeply about the matter and, later on he came to the Prophet, narrating his vision thus:

"When I was sleeping I saw a man with a bell in his hand, and I said "O Slave of God, will you please give me that bell?" He asked me what it was for and I explained that we are looking for some way of informing our people that the time for prayer had started. And he told me that it was not suitable for this purpose. Then he asked "Shall I teach you something you could use which would be suitable?" and I said, "Yes, Please".

Then he repeated the words of Adhan, as follows:-

Allahu Akbar (four times)
God is greatest.

Ashhadu an la ilaha illaha (twice)
I bear witness that there is no other deity than God.

Ashhadu Anna Muhammadan Rasulullah (twice)
Muhammad is the Messenger of God.

Hayy Ala al-Salah (twice)
Come to prayer

Hayy Ala al-Falah (twice)
Come to salvation

Allahu Akbar (twice)
God is greatest

La Illaha illallah
There is no other deity but God.

It was daytime, and he came to the Prophet to tell him about it as soon as possible. The Prophet, realising that this was indeed a vision asked the man to teach it to Bilal so that he would call it as his voice was the strongest. Bilal went to the roof of the mosque and repeated the words of the Adhan for the first time in the history of Islam. It is related, too, that Omar Ibn Al-Khattab heard the Adhan and ran towards the mosque quickly, saying:-

"I swear by God I have heard those words before, exactly as I hear them now".

There are a few words to be said here. The *Adhan* is a part of the worship in Islam, and it cannot be accepted as such unless it came to us by way of the Prophet. But how can it be said that it came from the Prophet, when it came through one of his companions? It is easy to explain this point, because certainly the Prophet received a revelation of the *Adhan* and he was waiting to inform his companions; and if they had a vision too there is no harm in accepting it because it is the truth. This event is remembered on the Day of *Adhan* in Islam.

THE DAY OF BADR

The Battle of Badr took place in the second year after Hijrah. It is important to know the background of this battle. The Prophet ordered his followers to emigrate from Makkah to Madinah and he followed them later on as was explained before. The people of Makkah didn't allow the followers to take their property with them; they took it away from them, by force, and used it for their own benefit, and also took their houses, farms and other possessions. But the Muslims left all these things and went to Madinah because it wasn't possible for them to practice faith among the people of Makkah, who always insulted them and inflicted harm upon them, and also killed some of them.

In the second year of Hijrah, the Prophet knew there was a trade caravan coming from Syria to Makkah, bearing goods belonging to the people of Makkah. He informed the companions, and they prepared themselves to go to stop this caravan, and to take the goods as recompense for the property which the people of Makkah had stolen. They had no intention of war.

The leader of the caravan knew in his own way that the Muslims were going to try to take his goods from him. So he sent a message to the people of Makkah asking for their protection. The people of Makkah came to his side – a gathering of over a thousand men prepared for war. The number of the Muslims was between 311 and 317, but before any encounter took place, the leader of the caravan escaped from the hand of the Muslims and met the people of Makkah, with all their property intact. He asked them to go back to Makkah, because there was no longer any reason to stay. But some of them, and one in particular called Abu Jahl insisted upon staying there for three days at a well called Badr, to drink and amuse himself and to threaten the Muslim people in order that they do not attempt the same thing again. When the Muslim people saw what was happening, they could not retreat, because this would have been a sign of weakness. In any case, if they did retreat, the people of Makkah might follow them to Madinah and fight them there.

The Prophet started to consult his companions. The majority of his companions were natives of Madinah, and a few of them were emigrants from Makkah. The Prophet said to them:

"Advise me, O people!"

When he said this, Abu Bakr stood up and gave his support. The Prophet thanked him and again repeated his call:-

"Advise me, O people!"

Then Omar gave his support. The Prophet thanked him and repeated again :-

"Advise me, O People".

Then one called Al Miqdad said:

"O Prophet, we will not speak to you as the Children of Israel spoke to Moses, saying "Go with your Lord to fight", and then remain behind and desert you. We will say "Go with your Lord and fight", and we stand by you wherever you go. By Allah, if you ask us to go anywhere, we will go".

But the Prophet again repeated his senetnce:

"Advise me, O people!"

It was clear that he was addressing the people of Madinah, because the three men who had answered were from Makkah.

Then the leader of the people of Madinah, Sad Ibn Muadh stood up and said:

*"O Prophet, it seems as if you mean us to answer
you. We believe in you and trust what you say and
we are witness that you have told us the truth.
Therefore, we give you our word and covenant to
obey and listen. O Prophet, O Messenger of Allah, go
– do what you will – we are with you. By Allah, who
sent you with the truth if you cross the sea we will
cross it with you, without any of us remaining behind.
And we are ready to meet our enemy tomorrow. We
are patient in war and we are steadfast in battle. May
Allah show you what will please you from us. Go,
with God's blessing, and we will follow you".*

When the Prophet heard that, he saw the expression
of joy in his face, and he said, "Go and be sure about the
tidings, for Allah has promised me victory"

Then the battle started, and most of the leaders of the
people of Makkah were killed – and they were defeated,
although their number was large and they had no shortage
of weapons, while the Muslims were few in number and
ill-armed: but they had faith in the cause.

There are many verses of the Holy Qur'an revealed
on this occasion, particularly in *Surat al Anfal* (8).

THE CONQUEST OF MAKKAH

On the 24th of Ramadan, in the 8th year of Hijrah, the
Prophet conquered Makkah. The reason for this was that
after his emigration to Madinah many battles took place
between him and the people of Makkah, who had
attacked the people of Madinah more than once. In the 6th
year of Hijrah the Prophet informed his companions that
he was going to Makkah to perform Umrah and they
accompanied him, bearing with them their sacrifice.

They went with no intention of making war, but when the Prophet and his followers approached Makkah they were refused entry, and the Makkan people stopped them from performing their Umrah. Then the Prophet sent one of his companions, Othman Ibn Affan, to explain to the people of Makkah that they hadn't come to make war, but to pay their respects to the House of God. But when the Messenger of the Prophet went to speak to the people, they kept him there for three days, and it was feared they had killed him. The Prophet became angry and made a covenant with his followers. If this rumour was true, they must fight the people of Makkah because of this terrible deed. The followers of the Prophet promised not to return home until they knew what had happened to the Messenger of the Prophet, and this day is known in Islamic history as the Day of *Baiat Al-Ridwan*. It is mentioned in the Holy Quran that on this day they pleased God in their sincerity and their readiness to make sacrifice in order to seek the truth.

Then the people of Makkah sent a delegation to the Prophet, returning at the same time his messenger. This delegation was sent to make an agreement between the people of Makkah and the Prophet.

They agreed that the Muslims must not enter Makkah this year, but that they would be permitted to enter next year. And the war must stop between both sides for ten years. Anyone who came to the people of Makkah from the side of the Prophet would not be allowed to return, but whoever came to the Prophet from Makkah must be allowed to return, and a further condition was that anyone wishing to form an alliance with the Prophet could do so, and anyone could form an alliance with the people of Makkah. When the Prophet's followers heard of these conditions they were not at all happy. They had no wish to go back to Madinah without paying their respects to the House of God in Makkah and they were surprised that the Prophet should be expected to return anyone coming from Makkah back to them, and yet not to have one of their people returned who had gone to the side of Makkah. They argued until Omar Ibn Al-Khattab became very angry and went to the Prophet, saying.

"Are we not in the right and they in the wrong ?"

The Prophet answered,

"Yes"

Then Omar said "But why should be accept this humiliation?"

The Prophet's answer was "I am the slave of God and His Messenger. He will never let me lose my way".

Omar could not continue talking to the Prophet after this. He went of Abu Bakr and expressed his sorrow for this. Abu Bakr explained to Omar that even if they didn't understand the benefits that this Agreement would bring them the Prophet certainly did know, and they must follow and put their trust in him. The Prophet saw the distress of his followers and he himself was saddened by it. He spoke to his wife, Omm Salamah about it, but she advised him to go a head with his sacrifice and start slaughtering the animals and that when they see him doing this they will follow him. Several events took place which made it clear that the Prophet's acceptance of the agreement had been of great benefit to the Muslim side, because it was the first time that the people of Makkah had accepted the existence of a Muslim community in Arabia, and other tribes could have an alliance with them if they wished, which had never been possible before. The other point which Muslim people could not understand was why they should return anyone who came from Makkah, and did not expect the Makkan people to return one from their side who had gone over to Makkah. The Prophet explained:

> "If anyone leaves us and goes to Makkah we don't want him back, because he is not with us. There will be no benefit in keeping anyone with us against his desire. But those who came from the side of Makkah, when we return them they will find a way of securing their freedom."

And this was so. Three people came from Makkah to the side of the Prophet. When the people of Makkah discovered this they sent a delegation to demand their return. The Prophet gave them the three people, and this caused a sad situation among the Muslim people. What happened when these three were being returned to Makkah? One of them, who was strong and brave killed one of the Makkans who had come to take him back, and the other two ran away. They stayed somewhere between Makkah and Syria, and when anyone came by from Makkan they stopped him and took away his property and made it very difficult for the Makkah people to carry on their trade. At last the Makkan people went to the

Prophet, asking him not to return anyone else who came
to him from their side. The Holy Quran, therefore, called
this agreement a great victory, because of the results which
came from it, and these verses of the Holy Quran were
revealed on this occasion:

> God's good pleasure was on the
> Believers when they swore fealty
> to thee under the tree; He knew
> what was in their hearts and he
> sent down tranquility to them;
> and he rewarded them with a speedy
> victory. And many gains will they
> acquire (besides) and God is
> exalted in Power, Full of wisdom.
> God has promised you many gains
> that he shall acquire, and He has
> given you these beforehand; and
> He has restrained the hands of
> men from you; that it may be a sign
> for the believers and that He may
> guide you to a straight path,
> and other gains (there are) which
> are not within your power, but
> which God has compassed. And God
> has power over all things.
>
> If the unbelievers should fight you,
> they would certainly turn their
> backs; then would they find neither
> protector nor helper.
> (Such has been) the practice (approved)
> of God already in the part; no change
> wilt thou find in the practice (approved) of God.
> And it is He Who has restrained their

Hands from you and your hands from them
in the midst of Makkah, after that He
Gave you the victory over them. And
God sees well all that you do.
They are the ones who denied
Revelation and hindered you
From the sacred Mosque and the
sacrificial animals, detained from
reaching their place of sacrifice.
Had there not been believing men
and believing women whom ye did
not know that ye were trampling
down and on whose account a crime
would have been accrued to you without
(your) knowledge, (God would have
allowed you to force your way, but
He held back your hands) that He
may admit to His mercy whom He will.
Apart, we should certainly have
Punished the unbelievers among them
With a grievous punishment.
While the Unbelievers got up in their
Hearts heat and cant – the heat and cant
of Ignorance – God sent down His tranquility
to His Apostle and to the Believers, and
made them stick close to the command of
self-restraint; and well were they
entitled to it and worthy of it. And God
has full knowledge of all things.
Truly did God fulfil the vision for
His Apostle; You shall enter the Sacred
Mosque, if God wills, with minds secure,
Heads shaved, hair cut short, and
without fear. For he knew what you
knew not, and He granted, besides this
a speedy victory.

It is He who sent His Apostle with
Guidance and the Religion of Truth, to
Proclaim it over all religion: and
enough is God for a Witness.

In the next year the Prophet came to Makkah with his companions to pay his respects to the House of God. Some time later a battle had taken place between two tribes, one of them allied to the people of Makkah. According to the Agreement the Makkan people had no right to help the allies but they did not keep away from the battle. They helped their allies and killed and allies of the Prophet. The allies of the Prophet explained to him what had happened and it was clear that the people of Makkah had broken their promise. Therefore the Prophet ordered his companions to be ready and they went to Makkah. They reached Makkah on the 24th Ramadan, in the eighth year of Al Hijrah. When the Prophet approached Makkah the news of his coming had reached the people before him, and they were in a difficult position. But the Prophet made an announcement:

"Whoever comes to the Mosque is saved and whoever stays at home and doesn't fight is also saved; whoever comes to the house of Abu Sufayan is also saved".

A large number of people did these things, but some of them insisted on fighting the Prophet and his companions. The battle did not last long and the Prophet and his companions entered Makkah. When the Prophet came to the House of God he prostrated himself and thanked God for what He had done for him, and he went around the House of God for *Tawaf* as a greeting to the house and asked for the key of the House, and went inside. He found the House full of idols. He broke all of them, saying the words:

"I bear witness there is no other deity than God".

He then prayed inside the house, and he ordered Bilal to stand on the roof and to call *Adhan* for the first time in the history of Makkah. This was a sign that Makkah was now in the hands of the Prophet, and the Makkan people were worried. They didn't know what the Prophet was going to do with them, because they remembered what they had done against him over the last twenty years. They remembered how they had harmed him and insulted him, how they had tried to kill and established a war against him, killed many of his followers and tried to destroy his town. All these things they remembered, having human nature as they did, and did not expect their lives to be spared. The Prophet, however, had not come to kill them, but to guide them into the right way and they sat in rows around the House of God, waiting, to discover their fate. Would they live or die? Then the Prophet came out of the House of God, stood at the doorway and directed his face towards them, saying:-

"Praise be to God who keeps his promise and gives victory to His servants and helps His army and defeats the enemies".

Then he said:-

"O People of Makkah! What do you expect me to do with you?"

And they answered:-

*"Something good. You are a noble brother and the
son of a noble brother."*

And the Prophet said:-

*"No harm shall befall you this day. Allah will forgive
you, He is a merciful benefactor. Go, you are free".*

What did the Prophet do? This was the act of one
who wanted to guide people in the right way, not to
destroy them. He came as a Messenger of God and his
call was to allow peace to prevail in the whole of Arabia.
And this was what made peace: he pardoned those who
had harmed him. And they did not forget his grace upon
them. Muslim historians, therefore, call this the Day of
Mercy. After this day the whole of Arabia opened its doors
to Islam, and there was nothing to stop Islam from
benefitting the lives of all Arabs tribes. Makkah, for them,
was now regarded as their capital. What Makkah
accepted, all Arabs would accept. When Makkah rejected,
all Arabs would reject; but there was now no chance that
Makkah would reject Islam.

THE FAREWELL PILGRIMAGE OF THE PROPHET

In the month of Dhu-Al-Qaadah, in the tenth year of
Hijra, the Prophet (peace be upon him) decided to go for
pilgrimage, and he made an announcement to the
Muslims, inviting them to join him. It is related that nearly
a hundred thousand Muslims from throughout Arabia
joined the Prophet on that pilgrimage.

When they arrived at Makkah, the Prophet stood on the Mountain of Arafat and addressed the Muslims. He gave a sermon which is known in Muslim history as the Farewell Speech, in which he emphasised many Islamic principles. We will cover this sermon in detail later.

It is related that the Day of Arafat fell that year on a Friday, and therefore they called it Al-Hajj al-Akbar, the Greatest Pilgrimage. Muslims always feel happy when the Day of Arafat falls on a Friday, because of the blessing of that day.

On that particular day the Prophet (peace be upon him) received the revelation of a verse from the Holy Quran which said that his mission was completed. Some Muslims, like Abu Bakr (may Allah bless him) understand this and could not keep themselves from crying.

This verse says:

> "This day have I perfected your religion for you, completed my favour upon you, and have chosen for you Islam as your religion".

When Abu Bakr heard this, he cried because he felt that the Prophet would soon leave this life.

In connection with this verse it is related that a Jewish man once said to Omar Ibn al-Khattab:

> "There is in your Book a verse, which, if it had been related about us, we should take the day on which it was revealed as a festival". And the man recited the verse. Omar answered:

> "By Allah, I know where and when that verse was revealed; we take the day in which it was revealed as

*two festivals, for it was revealed on the Day of Arafat,
and on Friday, both of which are festivals for every
Muslim".*

On that day when the Prophet was standing on Arafat
with the Muslims gathered round him, he mounted his
camel, and asked the people for their attention. He asked
someone to repeat what he had said to give a chance for
everyone to hear. He started his sermon by praising God
and said,

*"O people listen carefully to what I am going to tell
you, for I don't know, may be I will not meet you after
this in this place.*

*O people, know that robbery and bloodshed are not
proper for anyone.*

*You will soon see God, and He will question you about
your deeds.*

*The man with whom anything has been left in trust
must return to it its owner.*

You must renounce usury and theft once and for all......

*O people, Satan cannot hope hereafter that he will be
worshipped in your land. For the sake of your faith be
warned against him.*

The earth has come full circle and returned to the
shape and form that on the day of creation, the heavens
and the earth received.

The number of months in God's eyes is twelve, four

of which are sacred; They are Dhu Al-Qaadah, Dhu'l Hijjah and Muharram, which follow each other, and one single month, which is Rajab, which comes between Jomada and Shaban.

> *O people, you have rights over your wives, and your wives have rights over you. On your wives it is encumbent that they should not violate their conjugal faith, nor be guilty of any evil act. If they are so guilty, God permits you to send them away. Act kindly towards your wives, for they are prisoners in your hands and have no power of their own. You have taken them as a trust from God and by the words of God you have made them lawful for yourselves.*

Then people, use intelligence and wisdom in the understanding of the words I shall say to you. I have given you that which will always be your guide if you have recourse to it. That is the Book of God and the sayings of His Prophet.

> *O people, listen to my words and think deeply about them.*

Know that very Muslim is the brother of every other Muslim, and that all the Muslims are brothers one to another.

No property of a man is lawful for his brother unless it has been given him freely, so do not do injustice to yourselves.

> *"O God, have I truly proclaimed your commands?"*

> *"Yes, O Prophet of God", cried the gathering, "You have proclaimed to us the command of God".*

The Prophet then raised his eyes to heaven. "O God" he said, "Be my witness this day".

Another version of this sermon adds these sentences:

> "O people, all of you are children of Adam, and Adam was created from dust. There is no superiority for an Arab above a non-Arab, nor for a non-Arab above an Arab, or for a white above a non-white. All of you are equal. The men honoured in the sight of God are those who fear God most."

These are the main points which the Prophet touched on in his speech. The Prophet made it clear that usury is forbidden, bloodshed is forbidden and robbery is forbidden. The rights of wives are defined, and men must be just with their wives and must do good for them. Brotherhood and equality is the way of Islam, and the only way for people to be in good relationship with God is by their good deeds and pure hearts.

These important points were emphasised by the Prophet in the last year of his life, and he died nearly three months after this speech.

It is an example for us Muslims, to follow, and we should do our best to study the life and actions of the Prophet (peace be upon him), because they are a light to guide us.

PART IV

ISLAM

CHAPTER 4

Sources of Legislation in Islam

In Islam, there are certain sources through which one can find out the religious rules to deal with any matter. These sources are the Qur'an, the tradition of the Prophet (*Sunnah*), diligence (*Ijtihad*) and the agreement of whole nations on Particular matters. The root of relying on these sources is taken from the following tradition.

When the Prophet (peace be upon him) sent Muath to be the governor of the Yemen, he asked him: "What will you do if you come across a matter which needs you to give religious judgment? Muath replied: "I will judge according to what is written in the Holy Qur'an". Again the Prophet asked him: "Suppose you cannot find what you want in the Holy Qur'an? What will you do? "Muath replied: I will judge the matter according to the Sunnah of the Prophet". The Prophet then put another question to him saying: "If you do not find what you want in the sunnah, what are you going to do?" Then Muath replied: "I will do my best to give a fair judgment". The Prophet was pleased with his answer and expressed his pleasure saying: "Praise be to God who guides the messenger of His Prophet to do what would please him". From this tradition, Muslim jurists find out the rules for every aspect of their lives, whether it is of a worldly or religious nature. In addition to these three sources, they agree about one more. If a whole nation has the same opinion about a matter, this will be considered as one of the sources of legislation as well, and particularly the first generation of Islam.

It has been related that similar advice had been given to the governors who were sent after that by the *Khalifas*, such as Abu Bakr and Umar. The following pages will give a brief outline of the Qur'an and the Sunnah.

THE QUR'AN

The Holy Qur'an is the word of God, the Almighty as He revealed it to the Prophet Muhammad (peace be upon him). It is the last message from God, which was given to the last Prophet. The revelation lasted for only twenty three years. From the time when the Prophet was forty years of age until the day of his death.

The revelation came to the Prophet Muhammad in Makkah and at Madinah. The revelation received in Makkah is known as the Makkan revelation and that revealed in Madinah as the revelation of Madinah.

The Makkan revelation emphasizes the unity of God, and His might; and sets forth the belief in the Day of Resurrection, when people will be asked about their deeds in this life. It also draws the attention of mankind to the power of God through the circumstances of the creation of heaven and earth and it gives parables from the life of other nations and so draws the attention of the people of Makkah to the punishment these nations received from God because of their denial of Him. These parables are given in order to make the people of Makkah realize the punishment that could be incurred by denial of God and to make them think about the call of the Prophet Muhammad.

The revelation of Madinah gives much consideration to social life, to human relationships, family law and to systems of government. In general, we can say the rules for the relationships of Muslims to other members of the society and to the society as a whole are set out. And this revelation of Madinah also gives rules of the system of government in Islam and the economic relationship and internal relationship.

The Arabic form of Qur'an' is 'The speech of God, the Almighty'. Nobody, not even the Prophet Muhammad (peace be upon him), has the right to change one word of the Qur'an nor to add any word or to take one away. The arrangement of the Qur'an into chapters and verses has been done in accordance with the guidance of the Prophet Muhammad.

The Qur'an has been written down ever since it was first revealed. The Prophet Muhammad used to have a number of writer, who were known as the 'Writers of Revelation'. He used to tell them to write down the revelation he had received, and ordered then to put these writings in a certain place in a certain chapter. The Prophet used to teach the revelations to his companions by recitation. When they had learnt it they all used to recite the Qur'an by day and by night.

It was the habit of the Prophet to recite the Qur'an while the angle Gabriel listened to him, once during the month of Ramadan, but in the last year of his life he recited the Qur'an twice during the month of Ramadan with Gabriel.

When the Prophet died the Holy Qur'an was already written down and had been memorized in their hearts by a large number of his companions. When it was first written it was not written in one volume, because it was written on the bones of animals, on animal skins and the bark of trees; and it was kept by one of the wives of the Prophet, whose name was Hafsah.

After the Prophet's death Abu Bakr became a Khalif and at that time the Muslim people were subject to attacks from outside and from those who thought that Islam would come to an end after the death of the Prophet. Therefore the Muslims started to defend their land and their beliefs and there were many battles. In one of these battles, at Yamamah, a large number of Muslims who had memorized the Qur'an were killed. Umar ibn Alkhattab realised that there was a danger that all those who had memorized the Qur'an might be lost and that the knowledge of the Qur'an might therefore be affected.

He therefore discussed the matter with Abu Bakr as to whether the Holy Qur'an should be written in one volume so that it could be kept in safety and protected from loss, as he thought some more of those who had memorised it might be killed in other battle.

After consideration and some hesitation Abu Bakr agreed that it should be done. He and Umar Ibn Alkhattab sent for Zaid Ibn Thabit as he was the most gifted of the Revelation writers during the lifetime of the Prophet. They asked him to look for the Qur'an for it was written in various portions, and copy it into one volume. Zaid sent for the various portions which had been kept in a safe place and started to copy the Qur'an into one volume.

Zaid made one condition for this very responsible work. The condition was that he would not copy any verse unless he could find two of the companions who had memorized it from the Prophet in the same form as it was written in the old collection of sheets, thus making sure of its authenticity. This he did until he came to the verse number 127 of Chapter 9 of the Qur'an when he could find only one companion who had memorised it, so Zaid himself memorized it and considered himself the second companion to do so, and thus he fulfilled his condition. In this way the Qur'an was copied and made into one volume; and it has been kept safe up to the present day. So when we read the Qur'an nowadays, we read it exactly as the Prophet Muhammad received it at first, without addition or loss of any portion.

When a Muslim reads the Qur'an he considers himself to be worshipping, because he repeats the words of God. The Holy Qur'an is the first source of Islamic belief and law. It is the only book in the world which, up to the present, has had no change or addition made to it since it was revealed, fourteen hundred years ago. We Muslims believe that it will be preserved from change until the end of the world, because it contains a verse which says 'We have revealed the Holy Qur'an and certainly we will protect it and keep it safe'.

Here there are two examples. The first chapter 50 which was revealed in Makkah.

بِسْمِ اللهِ الرَّحْمٰنِ الرَّحِيْمِ ٥

In the name of Allah, Most Gracious, Most Merciful.

1. Qaf:
   By the Glorious Qur'an
   (Thou art Allah's Messenger).

   ١- قٓ ٥ وَالْقُرْاٰنِ الْمَجِيْدِ ٥

2. But they wonder that
   There has come to them
   A Warner from among
   Themselves.
   So the Unbelievers say:
   "A strange thing is this!

   ٢- بَلْ عَجِبُوْٓا اَنْ جَآءَهُمْ مُّنْذِرٌ
   مِّنْهُمْ فَقَالَ الْكٰفِرُوْنَ هٰذَا
   شَيْءٌ عَجِيْبٌ ٥

3. "What! When we die
   And become dust, (shall we
   Live again?) That is
   A (sort of) return
   Far (from our understanding)."

   ٣- ءَاِذَا مِتْنَا وَكُنَّا تُرَابًا ۚ ذٰلِكَ
   رَجْعٌ بَعِيْدٌ ٥

4. We already know
   How much of them
   The earth takes away:
   With Us is a record
   Guarding (the full account).

   ٤- قَدْ عَلِمْنَا مَا تَنْقُصُ الْاَرْضُ
   مِنْهُمْ ۚ
   وَعِنْدَنَا كِتٰبٌ حَفِيْظٌ ٥

5. But they deny the Truth
When it comes to them:
So they are in
A confused state.

٥۔ بَلْ كَذَّبُوْا بِالْحَقِّ لَمَّا جَآءَهُمْ فَهُمْ فِيْ أَمْرٍ مَّرِيْجٍ ٥

6. Do they not look
At the sky above them?—
How We have made it
And adorned it,
And there are no
Flaws in it?

٦۔ أَفَلَمْ يَنْظُرُوْا إِلَى السَّمَآءِ فَوْقَهُمْ كَيْفَ بَنَيْنَاهَا وَزَيَّنَّاهَا وَمَا لَهَا مِنْ فُرُوْجٍ ٥

7. And the earth—
We have spread it out,
And set thereon mountains
Standing firm, and produced
Therein every kind of
Beautiful growth (in pairs)—

٧۔ وَالْأَرْضَ مَدَدْنَاهَا وَأَلْقَيْنَا فِيْهَا رَوَاسِيَ وَأَنْبَتْنَا فِيْهَا مِنْ كُلِّ زَوْجٍ بَهِيْجٍ ٥

8. To be observed
And commemorated
By every devotee
Turning (to Allah).

٨۔ تَبْصِرَةً وَذِكْرَىٰ لِكُلِّ عَبْدٍ مُّنِيْبٍ ٥

9. And We send down
From the sky rain
Charged with blessing,
And We produce therewith
Gardens and Grain for harvests;

٩۔ وَنَزَّلْنَا مِنَ السَّمَآءِ مَآءً مُّبَارَكًا فَأَنْبَتْنَا بِهِ جَنَّاتٍ وَحَبَّ الْحَصِيْدِ ٥

10. And tall (and stately)
Palm-trees, with shoots
Of fruit-stalks, piled
One over another—

١٠۔ وَالنَّخْلَ بَاسِقَاتٍ لَّهَا طَلْعٌ نَّضِيْدٌ ٥

11. As sustenance for
(Allah's) Servants—
And We give (new) life
Therewith to land that is
Dead: Thus will be
The Resurrection.

١١۔ رِّزْقًا لِّلْعِبَادِ وَأَحْيَيْنَا بِهِ بَلْدَةً مَّيْتًا كَذٰلِكَ الْخُرُوْجُ ٥

12. Before them was denied
(The Hereafter) by the People
Of Noah, the Companions
Of the Rass, the Thamūd,

١٢۔ كَذَّبَتْ قَبْلَهُمْ قَوْمُ نُوْحٍ وَأَصْحَابُ الرَّسِّ وَثَمُوْدُ ٥

13. The 'Ād, Pharaoh,
    The brethren of Lūṭ,

۱۳- وَعَادٌ وَّفِرْعَوْنُ وَاِخْوَانُ لُوطٍ ۝

14. The Companions of the Wood,
    And the People of Tubba';
    Each one (of them) rejected
    The Messengers, and My warning
    Was duly fulfilled (in them).

۱۴- وَاَصْحٰبُ الْاَيْكَةِ وَقَوْمُ تُبَّعٍ ۚ
كُلٌّ كَذَّبَ الرُّسُلَ
فَحَقَّ وَعِيدِ ۝

15. Were We then weary
    With the first Creation,
    That they should be
    In confused doubt
    About a new Creation?

۱۵- اَفَعَيِينَا بِالْخَلْقِ الْاَوَّلِ ۭ
بَلْ هُمْ فِيْ لَبْسٍ
مِّنْ خَلْقٍ جَدِيْدٍ ۝

16. It was We Who
    Created man, and We know
    What dark suggestions his soul
    Makes to him: for We
    Are nearer to him
    Than (his) jugular vein.

۱۶- وَلَقَدْ خَلَقْنَا الْاِنْسَانَ
وَنَعْلَمُ مَا تُوَسْوِسُ بِهٖ نَفْسُهٗ ۚ وَنَحْنُ
اَقْرَبُ اِلَيْهِ مِنْ حَبْلِ الْوَرِيْدِ ۝

17. Behold, two (guardian angels)
    Appointed to learn (his doings)
    Learn (and note them),
    One sitting on the right
    And one on the left.

۱۷- اِذْ يَتَلَقَّى الْمُتَلَقِّيٰنِ
عَنِ الْيَمِيْنِ وَعَنِ الشِّمَالِ قَعِيْدٌ ۝

18. Not a word does he
    Utter but there is
    A sentinel by him,
    Ready (to note it).

۱۸- مَا يَلْفِظُ مِنْ قَوْلٍ
اِلَّا لَدَيْهِ رَقِيْبٌ عَتِيْدٌ ۝

19. And the stupor of death
    Will bring Truth (before
    His eyes): "This was
    The thing which thou
    Wast trying to escape!"

۱۹- وَجَاءَتْ سَكْرَةُ الْمَوْتِ بِالْحَقِّ ۭ
ذٰلِكَ مَا كُنْتَ مِنْهُ تَحِيْدُ ۝

20. And the Trumpet
    Shall be blown:
    That will be the Day
    Whereof Warning (had been
        given).

۲۰- وَنُفِخَ فِي الصُّوْرِ ۭ
ذٰلِكَ يَوْمُ الْوَعِيْدِ ۝

21. And there will come forth
Every soul: with each
Will be an (angel) to drive,
And an (angel) to
Bear witness.

٢١- وَجَآءَتْ كُلُّ نَفْسٍ مَعَهَا سَآئِقٌ وَشَهِيدٌ ○

22. (It will be said:)
"Thou wast heedless
Of this; now have We
Removed thy veil,
And sharp is thy sight
This Day!"

٢٢- لَقَدْ كُنْتَ فِيْ غَفْلَةٍ مِنْ هٰذَا فَكَشَفْنَا عَنْكَ غِطَآءَكَ فَبَصَرُكَ الْيَوْمَ حَدِيْدٌ ○

23. And his Companion will say:
"Here is (his Record) ready
With me!"

٢٣- وَقَالَ قَرِيْنُهٗ هٰذَا مَا لَدَيَّ عَتِيْدٌ ○

24. (The sentence will be:)
"Throw, throw into Hell
Every contumacious Rejecter
(Of Allah)! —

٢٤- أَلْقِيَا فِيْ جَهَنَّمَ كُلَّ كَفَّارٍ عَنِيْدٍ ○

25. "Who forbade what was good,
Transgressed all bounds,
Cast doubts and suspicions;

٢٥- مَنَّاعٍ لِلْخَيْرِ مُعْتَدٍ مُرِيْبٍ ○

26. "Who set up another god
Beside Allah: Throw him
Into a severe Penalty."

٢٦- الَّذِيْ جَعَلَ مَعَ اللهِ إِلٰهًا اٰخَرَ فَأَلْقِيٰهُ فِي الْعَذَابِ الشَّدِيْدِ ○

27. His Companion will say:
"Our Lord! I did not
Make him transgress,
But he was (himself)
Far astray."

٢٧- قَالَ قَرِيْنُهٗ رَبَّنَا مَآ أَطْغَيْتُهٗ وَلٰكِنْ كَانَ فِيْ ضَلٰلٍ بَعِيْدٍ ○

28. He will say: "Dispute not
With each other
In My Presence:
I had already in advance
Sent you Warning.

٢٨- قَالَ لَا تَخْتَصِمُوْا لَدَيَّ وَقَدْ قَدَّمْتُ إِلَيْكُمْ بِالْوَعِيْدِ ○

29. "The Word changes not
Before Me, and I do not
The least injustice
To My Servants."

٢٩- مَا يُبَدَّلُ الْقَوْلُ لَدَيَّ وَمَآ أَنَا بِظَلَّامٍ لِلْعَبِيْدِ ○

30. One Day We will
Ask Hell, "Art thou
Filled to the full?"
It will say, "Are there
Any more (to come)?"

٣٠- يَوْمَ نَقُولُ لِجَهَنَّمَ هَلِ
امْتَلَاتِ
وَتَقُولُ هَلْ مِنْ مَّزِيدٍ ۟

31. And the Garden
Will be brought nigh
To the Righteous— no more
A thing distant.

٣١- وَأُزْلِفَتِ الْجَنَّةُ
لِلْمُتَّقِينَ غَيْرَ بَعِيدٍ ۟

32. (A voice will say:)
"This is what was
Promised for you—
For everyone who turned
(To Allah) in sincere repentance,
Who kept (His Law),

٣٢- هٰذَا مَا تُوعَدُونَ
لِكُلِّ أَوَّابٍ حَفِيظٍ ۟

33. "Who feared (Allah)
Most Gracious unseen,
And brought a heart
Turned in devotion (to Him):

٣٣- مَنْ خَشِيَ الرَّحْمٰنَ بِالْغَيْبِ
وَجَاءَ بِقَلْبٍ مُّنِيبٍ ۟

34. "Enter ye therein
In Peace and Security;
This is a Day
Of Eternal Life!"

٣٤- ادْخُلُوهَا بِسَلَامٍ
ذٰلِكَ يَوْمُ الْخُلُودِ ۟

35. There will be for them
Therein all that they wish—
And more besides
In Our Presence.

٣٥- لَهُمْ مَّا يَشَاءُونَ فِيهَا
وَلَدَيْنَا مَزِيدٌ ۟

36. But how many
Generations before them
Did We destroy (for their
Sins)—stronger in power
Than they? Then did they
Wander through the land:
Was there any place
Of escape (for them)?

٣٦- وَكَمْ أَهْلَكْنَا قَبْلَهُمْ مِّنْ قَرْنٍ
هُمْ أَشَدُّ مِنْهُمْ بَطْشًا
فَنَقَّبُوا فِي الْبِلَادِ ۖ
هَلْ مِنْ مَّحِيصٍ ۟

37. Verily in this
    Is a Message
    For any that has
    A heart and understanding
    Or who gives ear and
    Earnestly witnesses (the truth).

٣٧۔ اِنَّ فِیۡ ذٰلِكَ لَذِكۡرٰی
لِمَنۡ كَانَ لَهٗ قَلۡبٌ
اَوۡ اَلۡقَی السَّمۡعَ وَهُوَ شَهِیۡدٌ ۰

38. We created the heavens
    And the earth and all
    Between them in Six Days,
    Nor did any sense
    Of weariness touch Us.

٣٨۔ وَلَقَدۡ خَلَقۡنَا السَّمٰوٰتِ وَ الۡاَرۡضَ
وَمَا بَیۡنَهُمَا فِیۡ سِتَّةِ اَیَّامٍ ۚ
وَّمَا مَسَّنَا مِنۡ لُّغُوۡبٍ ۰

39. Bear, then, with patience,
    All that they say,
    And celebrate the praises
    Of thy Lord, before
    The rising of the sun
    And before (its) setting.

٣٩۔ فَاصۡبِرۡ عَلٰی مَا یَقُوۡلُوۡنَ
وَسَبِّحۡ بِحَمۡدِ رَبِّكَ
قَبۡلَ طُلُوۡعِ الشَّمۡسِ وَقَبۡلَ
الۡغُرُوۡبِ ۚ

40. And during part
    Of the night, (also,)
    Celebrate His praises,
    And (so likewise)
    After the postures
    Of adoration.

٤٠۔ وَمِنَ الَّیۡلِ
فَسَبِّحۡهُ
وَ اَدۡبَارَ السُّجُوۡدِ۰

41. And listen for the Day
    When the Caller will call
    Out from a place
    Quite near—

٤١۔ وَاسۡتَمِعۡ یَوۡمَ یُنَادِ الۡمُنَادِ
مِنۡ مَّكَانٍ قَرِیۡبٍ ۚ

42. The Day when they will
    Hear a (mighty) Blast
    In (very) truth: that
    Will be the Day
    Of Resurrection.

٤٢۔ یَّوۡمَ یَسۡمَعُوۡنَ الصَّیۡحَةَ بِالۡحَقِّ ؕ
ذٰلِكَ یَوۡمُ الۡخُرُوۡجِ ۰

43. Verily it is We Who
    Give Life and Death;
    And to Us is
    The Final Goal—

٤٣۔ اِنَّا نَحۡنُ نُحۡیٖ وَنُمِیۡتُ
وَ اِلَیۡنَا الۡمَصِیۡرُ ۚ

44. The Day when
The Earth will be
Rent asunder, from (men)
Hurrying out: that will be
A gathering together—
Quite easy for Us.

يَوْمَ تَشَقَّقُ الْأَرْضُ عَنْهُمْ سِرَاعًا ٤٤ـ
ذٰلِكَ حَشْرٌ
عَلَيْنَا يَسِيرٌ ۝

45. We know best what they
Say; and thou art not
One to overawe them
By force. So admonish
With the Qur'ān such
As fear My Warning!

نَحْنُ أَعْلَمُ بِمَا يَقُولُونَ ٤٥ـ
وَمَا أَنْتَ عَلَيْهِمْ بِجَبَّارٍ
فَذَكِّرْ بِالْقُرْآنِ مَنْ يَخَافُ وَعِيدِ ۝

The second example is chapter 49 which was revealed at Madinah.

بِسْمِ اللهِ الرَّحْمٰنِ الرَّحِيمِ ۝

In the name of Allah, Most Gracious, Most Merciful.

1. O Ye who believe!
Put not yourselves forward
Before Allah and His Messenger;
But fear Allah: for Allah
Is He Who hears
And knows all things.

يَا أَيُّهَا الَّذِينَ آمَنُوا لَا تُقَدِّمُوا بَيْنَ ١ـ
يَدَيِ اللهِ وَرَسُولِهِ وَاتَّقُوا اللهَ
إِنَّ اللهَ سَمِيعٌ عَلِيمٌ ۝

2. O ye who believe!
Raise not your voices
Above the voice of the Prophet,
Nor speak aloud to him
In talk, as ye may
Speak aloud to one another,
Lest your deeds become
Vain and ye perceive not.

يَا أَيُّهَا الَّذِينَ آمَنُوا لَا تَرْفَعُوا ٢ـ
أَصْوَاتَكُمْ فَوْقَ صَوْتِ النَّبِيِّ وَلَا
تَجْهَرُوا لَهُ بِالْقَوْلِ كَجَهْرِ
بَعْضِكُمْ لِبَعْضٍ أَنْ تَحْبَطَ
أَعْمَالُكُمْ وَأَنْتُمْ لَا تَشْعُرُونَ ۝

3. Those that lower their voices
In the presence of
Allah's Messenger—their hearts
Has Allah tested for piety:
For them is Forgiveness
And a great Reward.

إِنَّ الَّذِينَ يَغُضُّونَ أَصْوَاتَهُمْ ٣ـ
عِنْدَ رَسُولِ اللهِ أُولَٰئِكَ الَّذِينَ
امْتَحَنَ اللهُ قُلُوبَهُمْ لِلتَّقْوٰى
لَهُمْ مَغْفِرَةٌ وَأَجْرٌ عَظِيمٌ ۝

4. Those who shout out
   To thee from without
   The Inner Apartments—
   Most of them lack understanding.

٣- اِنَّ الَّذِيْنَ يُنَادُوْنَكَ مِنْ وَّرَآءِ الْحُجُرٰتِ اَكْثَرُهُمْ لَا يَعْقِلُوْنَ ۝

5. If only they had patience
   Until thou couldst
   Come out to them,
   It would be best
   For them: but Allah is
   Oft-Forgiving, Most Merciful.

٥- وَلَوْ اَنَّهُمْ صَبَرُوْا حَتّٰى تَخْرُجَ اِلَيْهِمْ لَكَانَ خَيْرًا لَّهُمْ ۫ وَاللّٰهُ غَفُوْرٌ رَّحِيْمٌ ۝

6. O ye who believe!
   If a wicked person comes
   To you with any news,
   Ascertain the truth, lest
   Ye harm people unwittingly,
   And afterwards become
   Full of repentance for
   What ye have done.

٦- يٰٓاَيُّهَا الَّذِيْنَ اٰمَنُوْٓا اِنْ جَآءَكُمْ فَاسِقٌ بِنَبَاٍ فَتَبَيَّنُوْٓا اَنْ تُصِيْبُوْا قَوْمًا بِجَهَالَةٍ فَتُصْبِحُوْا عَلٰى مَا فَعَلْتُمْ نٰدِمِيْنَ ۝

7. And know that among you
   Is Allah's Messenger: were he,
   In many matters, to follow
   Your (wishes), ye would
   Certainly fall into misfortune:
   But Allah has endeared
   The Faith to you, and
   Has made it beautiful
   In your hearts, and He
   Has made hateful to you
   Unbelief, wickedness, and
   Rebellion: such indeed are
   Those who walk in
   righteousness;—

٧- وَاعْلَمُوْٓا اَنَّ فِيْكُمْ رَسُوْلَ اللّٰهِ ۭ لَوْ يُطِيْعُكُمْ فِيْ كَثِيْرٍ مِّنَ الْاَمْرِ لَعَنِتُّمْ وَلٰكِنَّ اللّٰهَ حَبَّبَ اِلَيْكُمُ الْاِيْمَانَ وَزَيَّنَهُ فِيْ قُلُوْبِكُمْ وَكَرَّهَ اِلَيْكُمُ الْكُفْرَ وَالْفُسُوْقَ وَالْعِصْيَانَ ۭ اُولٰٓئِكَ هُمُ الرّٰشِدُوْنَ ۙ

8. A Grace and Favour
   From Allah; and Allah
   Is full of Knowledge
   And Wisdom.

٨- فَضْلًا مِّنَ اللّٰهِ وَنِعْمَةً ۭ وَاللّٰهُ عَلِيْمٌ حَكِيْمٌ ۝

9. If two parties among
The Believers fall into
A quarrel, make ye peace
Between them: but if
One of them transgresses
Beyond bounds against the other,
Then fight ye (all) against
The one that transgresses
Until it complies with
The command of Allah;
But if it complies, then
Make peace between them
With justice, and be fair:
For Allah loves those
Who are fair (and just).

وَاِنْ طَآئِفَتٰنِ مِنَ الْمُؤْمِنِيْنَ
اقْتَتَلُوْا فَاَصْلِحُوْا بَيْنَهُمَا ۚ
فَاِنْ بَغَتْ اِحْدٰىهُمَا عَلَى الْاُخْرٰى
فَقَاتِلُوا الَّتِىْ تَبْغِىْ
حَتّٰى تَفِىْٓءَ اِلٰٓى اَمْرِ اللّٰهِ ۚ
فَاِنْ فَآءَتْ
فَاَصْلِحُوْا بَيْنَهُمَا بِالْعَدْلِ
وَاَقْسِطُوْا ۚ
اِنَّ اللّٰهَ يُحِبُّ الْمُقْسِطِيْنَ ۝

10. The Believers are but
A single Brotherhood:
So make peace and
Reconciliation between your
Two (contending) brothers;
And fear Allah, that ye
May receive Mercy.

١٠۔ اِنَّمَا الْمُؤْمِنُوْنَ اِخْوَةٌ
فَاَصْلِحُوْا بَيْنَ اَخَوَيْكُمْ
وَاتَّقُوا اللّٰهَ لَعَلَّكُمْ تُرْحَمُوْنَ ۝

11. O ye who believe!
Let not some men
Among you laugh at others:
It may be that
The (latter) are better
Than the (former):
Nor let some women
Laugh at others:
It may be that
The (latter) are better
Than the (former):
Nor defame nor be
Sarcastic to each other,
Nor call each other
By (offensive) nicknames:
Ill-seeming is a name
Connoting wickedness,
(To be used of one)
After he has believed:
And those who
Do not desist are
(Indeed) doing wrong.

١١۔ يٰٓاَيُّهَا الَّذِيْنَ اٰمَنُوْا
لَا يَسْخَرْ قَوْمٌ مِّنْ قَوْمٍ
عَسٰٓى اَنْ يَّكُوْنُوْا خَيْرًا مِّنْهُمْ
وَلَا نِسَآءٌ مِّنْ نِّسَآءٍ
عَسٰٓى اَنْ يَّكُنَّ خَيْرًا مِّنْهُنَّ ۚ
وَلَا تَلْمِزُوْٓا اَنْفُسَكُمْ
وَلَا تَنَابَزُوْا
بِالْاَلْقَابِ ۚ
بِئْسَ الِاسْمُ الْفُسُوْقُ
بَعْدَ الْاِيْمَانِ ۚ
وَمَنْ لَّمْ يَتُبْ
فَاُولٰٓئِكَ هُمُ الظّٰلِمُوْنَ ۝

12. Ⓞ ye who believe!
    Avoid suspicion as much
    (As possible): for suspicion
    In some cases is a sin:
    And spy not on each other
    Behind their backs. Would any
    Of you like to eat
    The flesh of his dead
    Brother? Nay, ye would
    Abhor it...But fear Allah:
    For Allah is Oft-Returning,
    Most Merciful.

13. Ⓞ mankind! We created
    You from a single (pair)
    Of a male and a female,
    And made you into
    Nations and tribes, that
    Ye may know each other
    (Not that ye may despise
    Each other). Verily
    The most honoured of you
    In the sight of Allah
    Is (he who is) the most
    Righteous of you.
    And Allah has full knowledge
    And is well acquainted
    (With all things).

14. The desert Arabs say,
    "We believe." Say, "Ye
    Have no faith; but ye
    (Only) say, 'We have
                submitted
    Our wills to Allah,'
    For not yet has Faith
    Entered your hearts.
    But if ye obey Allah
    And His Messenger, He
    Will not belittle aught
    Of your deeds: for Allah
    Is Oft-Forgiving, Most Merciful."

۱۲- يَاۤيُّهَا الَّذِيْنَ اٰمَنُوا
اجْتَنِبُوْا كَثِيْرًا مِّنَ الظَّنِّ ۫
اِنَّ بَعْضَ الظَّنِّ اِثْمٌ وَّلَا تَجَسَّسُوْا

وَلَا يَغْتَبْ بَّعْضُكُمْ بَعْضًا ؕ
اَيُحِبُّ اَحَدُكُمْ اَنْ يَّاْكُلَ لَحْمَ اَخِيْهِ
مَيْتًا فَكَرِهْتُمُوْهُ ؕ وَاتَّقُوا اللّٰهَ ؕ
اِنَّ اللّٰهَ تَوَّابٌ رَّحِيْمٌ۞

۱۳- يَاۤيُّهَا النَّاسُ اِنَّا خَلَقْنٰكُمْ
مِّنْ ذَكَرٍ وَّاُنْثٰى
وَجَعَلْنٰكُمْ شُعُوْبًا
وَّ قَبَآئِلَ لِتَعَارَفُوْا ؕ
اِنَّ اَكْرَمَكُمْ
عِنْدَ اللّٰهِ اَتْقٰىكُمْ ؕ
اِنَّ اللّٰهَ عَلِيْمٌ خَبِيْرٌ۞

۱۴- قَالَتِ الْاَعْرَابُ
اٰمَنَّا ؕ قُلْ لَّمْ تُؤْمِنُوْا
وَلٰكِنْ قُوْلُوْۤا اَسْلَمْنَا
وَلَمَّا يَدْخُلِ الْاِيْمَانُ فِيْ
قُلُوْبِكُمْ ؕ
وَاِنْ تُطِيْعُوا اللّٰهَ وَرَسُوْلَهُ
لَا يَلِتْكُمْ مِّنْ اَعْمَالِكُمْ شَيْئًا ؕ
اِنَّ اللّٰهَ غَفُوْرٌ رَّحِيْمٌ۞

15. Only those are Believers
Who have believed in Allah
And His Messenger, and have
Never since doubted, but
Have striven with their
Belongings and their persons
In the Cause of Allah:
Such are the sincere ones,

١٥- اِنَّمَا الْمُؤْمِنُوْنَ الَّذِيْنَ اٰمَنُوْا بِاللّٰهِ وَرَسُوْلِهٖ ثُمَّ لَمْ يَرْتَابُوْا وَجَاهَدُوْا بِاَمْوَالِهِمْ وَاَنْفُسِهِمْ فِيْ سَبِيْلِ اللّٰهِ ؕ اُولٰٓئِكَ هُمُ الصّٰدِقُوْنَ۞

16. Say: "What! Will ye
Instruct Allah about your
Religion? But Allah knows
All that is in the heavens
And on earth: He has
Full knowledge of all things.

١٦- قُلْ اَتُعَلِّمُوْنَ اللّٰهَ بِدِيْنِكُمْ ؕ وَاللّٰهُ يَعْلَمُ مَا فِى السَّمٰوٰتِ وَمَا فِى الْاَرْضِ ؕ وَاللّٰهُ بِكُلِّ شَىْءٍ عَلِيْمٌ۞

17. They impress on thee
As a favour that they
Have embraced Islam.
Say, "Count not your Islam
As a favour upon me:
Nay, Allah has conferred
A favour upon you
That He has guided you
To the Faith, if ye
Be true and sincere.

١٧- يَمُنُّوْنَ عَلَيْكَ اَنْ اَسْلَمُوْا ؕ قُلْ لَّا تَمُنُّوْا عَلَيَّ اِسْلَامَكُمْ ۚ بَلِ اللّٰهُ يَمُنُّ عَلَيْكُمْ اَنْ هَدٰىكُمْ لِلْاِيْمَانِ اِنْ كُنْتُمْ صٰدِقِيْنَ۞

18. "Verily Allah knows [4938]
The secrets of the heavens
And the earth: and Allah
Sees well all
That ye do."

١٨- اِنَّ اللّٰهَ يَعْلَمُ غَيْبَ السَّمٰوٰتِ وَالْاَرْضِ ؕ وَاللّٰهُ بَصِيْرٌ بِمَا تَعْمَلُوْنَ۞

THE SUNNAH

Sunnah means the Prophet's sayings and what he did, and what his Companions did, to which he showed no objection. There are three things dealt with in this range-speech, action and the acceptance of action by others. Sometime we say Hadith and mean what the prophet said to his Companions about the matters of practices, beliefs and other things dealing with the manner of living. An example of this is the saying of the Prophet 'Fear God wherever you are and let the good deed follow the bad deed in order to abolish it, and deal with people of good character'. Another saying of the Prophet is "The likeness between a good friend and a bad friend is the likeness between a perfume seller and a smith. The one who sells perfume, if you accompany him may be will give you some of his perfume, or may be you will buy from him or you will get a good smell of it. If you accompany the smith the sparks from his fire may burn you and the smoke which comes out when he uses the bellows may harm you'.

The second kind of Sunnah deals with the action of the Prophet such as the way of performing prayer, ablutions, pilgrimage and other relative matters.

The third kind of Sunnah, is the acceptance of what other people have done such as having seen some of his Companions doing or saying what was not objectionable in the sight of the Prophet. These three kinds of Sunnah are all attributed to the Prophet(peace be upon him).

The Sunnah is the second source of Islamic belief and law, and the first source is the Qur'an. The Sunnah is to the Qur'an an explanation or interpretation. We have been ordered by the Qur'an to follow the Sunnah of the Prophet and it is obligatory to carry out the instructions given in the Sunnah for the Holy Qur'an says "What the Prophet ordered you to do you have to do and keep away from what he prohibited you to do". Another saying from the Qur'an is 'But no, by Thy Lord, they can have no(real) faith until they make Thee judge in all disputed between them and find in their souls no resistance against they decisions, but accept them with the fullest conviction'.

The Sunnah comes after the Qur'an as is understood from some Hadith and actions of the Companions of the Prophet. The Prophet once sent Muadh Ibn Jabal to Yamen and asked him how he would judge between people. Muadh answered 'When I am faced with the problem I will look through the Book of God, the Qur'an. If I get a decision from the Qur'an I will take it'. The Prophet said ' If you do not find what you are looking for what will you do? Muadh said 'Then I will look through the Sunnah of the Prophet'. The Prophet asked again 'If you do not find in the Sunnah what you are looking for? 'Muadh said 'I will do my best to give a fair judgement'. It is also understood from the letter which has been written byUmar, the second Khalipha to Shurayh: 'When you receive my letter, judge between people according to the Book of God. If you face a problem about which there is nothing in the 'Qur'an then judge between people according to the Sunnah of the Prophet'. This has been said by many of the Companions of the Prophet and it gives them to understand that the Sunah of the Prophet comes after the Qur'an.

Muslims, from the beginning, paid great care and attention to the Sunnah of the Prophet. They used to listen to his guidance and instructions with concentration so that they could explain to others what they had heard from the Prophet as he had said to them, One of his sayings was.' God blesses one who has heard it from me. Maybe the one who hears it from him will be more careful then him'.

After the first generation who lived with the Prophet the next generation also gave much care to the Sunnah of the Prophet. Each one tried to find out what the Prophet had said and to transmit it. The sayings of the Prophet in every area was like a shining light or guidance to people. They gathered round those who had heard the Prophet speaking so as to receive guidance from them. Thus a group of people was established in the Muslim community who were known as *Muhaddthun* (Transmitters).

After the Muslim state became widely established many countries accepted Islam, and people mixed with each other. Some of them were not really Muslims but tried to show the people that they were, in order to get a chance to corrupt Islam. Therefore these people started to attribute to the Prophet things he did not say. When Muslim scholars discovered this they set up rules for the study of Sunnah and many other branches of knowledge. Also a study was established to deal with the people who transmitted the sayings of the Prophet so as to find out about their character, particularly their honesty and trustworthiness, their ability to think clearly and whether in fact they had actually met the people from whom they said they had received the Sunnah. As a result of these enquiries many people failed to pass the test.

Thus, a new science in Islam was established known as *Ilm Alrigal* (the knowledge of the character of the people). The names of the Transmitters the date of their birth, the date of their death and manes of their teachers from whom they received the Sunnah, the places to which they had gone, their general character, belief and attitude towards others were all studied. They would them examine what a man said heard from other people. If they believed it was acceptable they could give a decision saying that his authority could be accepted with regard to the Sunnah.

In the Second century of Islam Muslim scholars made a study of collecting the sayings of the Prophet and, later on, at the end of the Second century and at the beginning of the Third, the School of Hadith gave us well known scholars as Al-Bukhari, Muslim, Al-Tirmidhi, and others. Thus it continues up to the present time. One can still look up the records of anyone in the field of Sunnah who has been examined by these scholars, and find out if they had or had not, been given authority to transmit the Sunnah and you can also get a report saying whether what he transmitted had actually been said by the Prophet or not.

GUARDING THE TONGUE FROM SLANDER AND ABUSE

Sahl b. Sa'd reported God's Messenger as saying, "If

anyone guarantees me what is between his legs, I shall guarantee him Paradise".

عَنْ سَهْلِ بْنِ سَعْدٍ قَالَ: قَالَ رَسُولُ اللهِ صَلَّى اللهُ عَلَيْهِ وَسَلَّمَ: مَنْ يَضْمَنُ لِي مَا بَيْنَ رِجْلَيْهِ أَضْمَنُ لَهُ الْجَنَّةَ.

Abu Huraira reported God's messenger as saying, "A man speaks a word pleasing to God without considering it of any importance, yet God exalts him several grades for it; another speaks a word displeasing to God without considering it of any importance, yet for it he will sink down into *jahannam*". Bukhari transmitted it. A version by Bukhari and Muslim says he will sink down for it into hell farther than the distance between the east and the west.

عَنْ أَبِي هُرَيْرَةَ قَالَ: قَالَ رَسُولُ اللهِ صلى اللهُ عَلَيْهِ وَسَلَّم: إِنَّ الْعَبْدَ لَيَتَكَلَّمُ بِالْكَلِمَةِ مِنْ رِضْوَانِ اللهِ لاَ يُلْقَى لَهَا بَالاً، يَرْفَعُ اللهُ بِهَا دَرَجَاتٍ، وَإِنَّ الْعَبْدَ لَيَتَكَلَّمُ بِالْكَلِمَةِ مِنْ سَخَطِ اللهِ لاَ يُلْقَى لَهَا بَالاً يَهْوِى بِهَا فِي جَهَنَّمَ. وَفِيْ رِوَايَةٍ: يَهْوِى بِهَا فِي النَّارِ أَبْعَدُ مَا بَيْنَ الْمَشْرِقِ وَالْمَغْرِبِ.

KINDNESS, AND JOINING TIES OF RELATIONSHIP

Abu Huraira told that a man said, "Messenger of God, who is most deserving of friendly care from me?"

He replied, "Your mother". He asked who came next and he replied, "Your mother". He asked who came next and he replied, "Your father". In another version he replied, "your mother, then, your mother, then your mother and then your father and then your nearest relatives in order".

عَنْ أَبِي هُرَيْرَةَ قَالَ: قَالَ رَجُلٌ: يَا رَسُولُ اللهِ مَنْ أَحَقُّ بِحُسْنِ صُحْبَتِي؟ قَالَ: اُمُّكَ، قَالَ: ثُمَّ مَنْ؟ قَالَ :اُمُّكَ، قَالَ: ثُمَّ مَنْ؟ قَالَ: اُمُّكَ، قَالَ: ثُمَّ مَنْ؟ قَالَ: أَبُوكَ.

وَفِي رِوَايَةٍ قَالَ: اُمُّكَ، ثُمَّ اُمُّكَ، ثُمَّ اُمُّكَ، ثُمَّ أَبَاكَ، ثُمَّ ادْنَاكَ ادْنَاكَ

Abu Huraira reported God's messenger as saying that when God had finished creating all things, ties of relationship arose and seized the loins of the Compassionate One. He said, "Stop!" and they said, "This is the place for him who seeks refuge in thee from being cut off". He replied "Are you not satisfied that I should keep connection with him who keeps you united and sever connection with him who severs you?" They said, "O certainly, Lord." And He replied, " Well, that is how things are".

عَنْ أَبِي هُرَيْرَةَ قَالَ: قَالَ رَسُولُ اللهِ صَلَّى اللهُ عَلَيْهِ وَسَلَّمَ: خَلَقَ اللهُ الْخَلْقَ، فَلَمَّا فَرَغَ مِنْهُ قَامَتِ الرَّحْمُ، فَأَخَذَتْ بِحَقْوَى الرَّحْمَنِ، فَقَالَ: مَهْ، قَالَتْ: هَذَا مَقَامُ الْعَائِذِ بِكَ مِنَ الْقَطِيعَةِ، قَالَ: اَلاَ تَرْضَيْنَ اَنْ أَصِلَ مَنْ وَصَلَكِ، وَاَقْطَعَ مَنْ قَطَعَكِ؟ قَالَتْ: بَلَى يَا رَبِّ، قَالَ فَذَاكِ.

Abu Huraira told that a man said, "Messenger of God, I have relatives with whom I try to unite ties of relationship but who sever relations with me, whom I treat kindly but who treat me badly, with whom I am gentle but who are rough to me". He ashes to them, and you will not be without a support against them from God as along as you do so".

وَعَنْ اَبِيْ هُرَيْرَةَ اَنَّ رَجُلاً قَالَ:يَا رَسُولَ اللهِ إِنَّ لِيْ قَرَابَةً اصِلُهُمْ
وَيَقْطَعُوني وَ أَحْسِنُ إِلَيْهِمْ وَيُسِيْئُونَ إِلَيَّ واحْلُمُ عَنْهُمْ وَيَجْهَلُونَ
عَلَيَّ. فَقَالَ: لَئِنْ كُنْتَ كَمَا قُلْتَ فَكَأَنَّمَا تسفهم الملّ،وَلاَ يَزَالُ
مَعَكَ مِنَ اللهِ ظَهِيرٌ عَلَيْهِمْ مَا دُمْتَ عَلَى ذَلِكِ.

GENTLENESS, MODESTY AND GOOD CHARACTER

Aisha reported God's messenger as saying, "God is gentle and likes gentleness. He gives for gentleness what He does not give for harshness and what He does not give for anything else". Muslim transmitted it. In a version by him he said to Aisha, "keep to gentleness and avoid harshness and coarseness. Gentleness is not found in anything without adorning it, and is not withdrawn from anything without shaming it".

عَنْ عَائِشَةَ رضِيَ اللهُ عَنْهَا أَنَّ رَسُولَ اللهِ صَلَّى اللهُ عَلَيْهِ وَسَلَّمَ قَالَ:
إِنَّ اللهَ تَعَالَى رَفِيْقٌ يُحِبُّ الرِّفْقَ، وَيُعْطِي عَلَى الرِّفْقِ مَالاَ يُعْطِي

عَلَى الْعُنْفِ، وَمَا لاَ يُعْطِي عَلَى مَا سِوَاه.

وَفِيْ رِوَايَةٍ: عَلَيْكَ بِالرِّفْقِ، وَإِيَاكَ وَالْعُنْفَ وَالْفَحْشَ، إِنَّ الرِّفْقَ

لاَ يَكُونُ فِي شَئٍ إِلاَّ زَانَه، وَلاَ يُنْزَعُ مِنْ شَئٍ إِلا شَانَه.

Jabir reported the Prophet as saying, "He who is given his portion of the gentleness is given the good in this world and in the next and He who is deprived of gentleness is deprived of good in this world and in the next".

مَنْ أُعْطِيَ حَظَّهُ مِنَ الرِّفْقِ أُعْطِيَ حَظَّه مِنْ خَيْرِ الدُّنْيَا وَالآخِرَة

وَمَنْ حُرِمَ حَظَّهُ مِنَ الرِّفْقِ حُرِمَ حَظَّهُ مِنْ خَيْرِ الدُّنْيَا وَالآخِرَة.

ANGER AND PRIDE

Abu Huraira told that a man asked the Prophet to give him some instruction and he said, " Do not be angry". The man repeated that several times and he replied, " Do not be angry".

عَنْ ابِيْ هُرَيْرَةَ أَنَّ رَجُلاً قَالَ لِلنَّبِي صَلَّى اللهُ عَلَيْهِ وَسَلَّمَ: اَوْصِنِيْ،

قَالَ: لاَ تَغْضَبْ، فَرَدَّدَ ذَلِكَ مِرَاراً، قَالَ لاَ تَغْضَبْ.

He reported God's messenger as saying, "The strong

man is not the good wrestler; the strong man is only he
who controls himself when he is angry".

عَنْ أَبِي هُرَيْرَةَ قَالَ: قَالَ رَسُولُ اللهِ صلَّى اللهُ عَلَيْهِ وَسَلَّمَ: لَيْسَ
الشَّدِيدُ بِالصَّرْعَةِ، إِنَّمَا الشَّدِيدُ الَّذِي يَمْلِكُ نَفْسَهُ عِنْدَ الْغَضَبِ.

Ibn Mis'ud reported God's messenger as saying, "He
who has in his heart as much faith as a grain of mustard
seed will not enter hell, and he who has in his heart as
much pride as a grain of mustard seed will not enter
paradise".

عَنِ ابْنِ مَسْعُودٍ قَالَ: قَالَ رَسُولُ اللهِ صَلَّى اللهُ عَلَيْهِ وَسَلَّمَ:
لاَ يَدْخُلُ النَّارَ أَحَدٌ فِيْ قَلْبِهِ مِثْقَالُ حَبَّةٍ مِنْ خَرْدَلٍ مِنْ إِيْمَانٍ
وَلاَ يَدْخُلُ الْجَنَّةَ أَحَدٌ فِيْ قَلْبِهِ مِثْقَالُ حَبَّةٍ مِنْ خَرْدَلٍ مِنْ كِبْرٍ.

Abu Huraira reported God's messenger as saying,
"There are three types to whom God will not speak on
the day of resurrection and whom He will not purify (a
version has, 'and at whom He will not look'), and they
will have a painful punishment: An old man who commits
fornication, a king who is a great liar, and a poor man
who is proud".

عَنْ أَبِيْ هُرَيْرَةَ قَالَ: قَالَ رَسُولُ اللهِ صَلَّى اللهُ عَلَيْهِ وَسَلَّمَ: ثَلاَثَةٌ
لاَ يُكَلِّمُهُمُ اللهُ يَوْمَ الْقِيَامَةِ وَلاَ يُزَكِّيْهِمْ، وَفِيْ رِوَايَةٍ: وَلاَ يَنْظُرُ اَلَيْهِمْ
وَلَهُمْ عَذَابٌ أَلِيْمٌ: شَيْخٌ زَانٍ، وَمَلِكٌ كَذَّابٌ، وَعَائِلٌ مُسْتَكْبِرٌ.

He reported God's messenger as stating that God most high says, "Pride is my cloak and majesty is my lower garment, and I shall cause him who vies with me regarding one of them to enter Hell". A version has, "I shall throw him into hell".

عَنْ اَبِي هُرَيْرَةَ قَالَ: قَالَ رَسُولُ الله صَلَّى الله عَلَيْهِ وَسَلَّمَ: يَقُولُ اللهُ تَعَالَى: الْكِبْرِيَاءُ رِدَائِي، وَالْعَظْمَةُ اِزَارِي فَمَنْ نَازَعَنِيْ وَاحِداً مِنْهُمَا ادْخَلْتُهُ النَّارَ، وَفِيْ رِوَايَةٍ قَذَفْتُهُ فِي النَّارِ.

GOOD ACTION AND MORALS

Ibn Mas'ud reported God's messenger as saying, "Two people only may be envied: a man to whom God has given property, empowering him to dispose of it on what is right; and a man to whom God has given wisdom who acts according to it and teaches it".

عَنِ ابْنِ مَسْعُودٍ قَالَ: قَالَ رَسُولُ الله صَلَّى الله عَلَيهِ وَسَلَّمَ: لاَ حَسدَ الاَّ فِي اثْنَتَيْنِ: رَجُلٌ اَتَاهُ اللهُ مَالاً فسلَّطَه عَلَى هَلَكَتِهِ فِي الْحَقِّ، وَرَجُلٌ اَتَاهُ اللهُ الْحِكْمَةَ فَهُوَ يَعْمَلُ بِهَا وَيُعَلِّمُهَا النَّاسَ.

Abu Huraira reported God's messenger as saying, "When a man dies no further reward is recorded for his actions, with three exceptions: *sadaqa* which continues to be supplied, or knowledge from which benefit continues

to be reaped , or the prayers of a good son for his dead
father".

عَنْ اَبِي هُرَيْرَةَ قَالَ: قَالَ رَسُولُ اللهِ صلَّى اللهُ عَلَيْهِ وَسَلَّمَ: اذَا مَاتَ
الانْسَانُ انْقَطَعَ عَمَلُهُ إلا مِنْ ثَلاَثَةَ اشْيَاءَ: صَدَقَةٍ جَارِيَةٍ، اَوْ عِلْمٍ
يُنْتَفَعُ بِهِ أو وَلَدٍ صَالِحٍ يَدْعُو لَهُ.

He also reported God's messenger as saying, "If
anyone removes one of the anxieties of this world from
a believer, God will remove one of the anxieties of the
day of resurrection from him; if one smooths the way for
one who is destitute, God will smooth the way for him
in this world and the next; and if anyone conceals the
faults of a Muslim, God will conceal his faults in this
world and the next. God helps a man as long as he helps
his brother. If anyone pursues a path in search of
knowledge, God will thereby make easy for him a path
to paradise. No company will gather in a mosque to recite
God's Book and study it together without calmness
descending on them, mercy covering them, the angels
surrounding them, and God mentioning' them among
those who are with Him. But he who is made slow by his
actions will not be speeded by his genealogy,".

عَنْ أبِي هُرَيْرَةَ قَالَ: قَالَ رَسُولُ اللهِ صَلَّى اللهُ عَلَيْهِ وَسَلَّمَ: مَنْ نَفَّسَ
عَنْ مُؤْمِنٍ كُرْبَةً مِنْ كُرَبِ الدُّنْيَا نَفَّسَ اللهُ عَنْهُ كُرْبَةً مِنْ كُرَبِ يَوْمِ
الْقِيَامَةِ، وَمَنْ يَسَّرَ عَلَى مُعْسِرٍ يَسَّرَ اللهُ عَلَيْهِ فِيْ الدُّنْيَا والآخِرَةِ، وَمَنْ

سَتَرَ مُسْلِمًا سَتَرَهُ اللهُ فِي الدُّنْيَا وَالآخِرَةِ، وَاللهُ فِي عَوْنِ الْعَبْدِ مَا كَانَ
الْعَبْدُ فِي عَوْنِ أَخِيْهِ، وَ مَنْ سَلَكَ طَرِيقاً يَلْتَمِسُ فِيْهِ عِلْمًا سَهَّلَ اللهُ لَهُ
بِهِ طَرِيْقًا اِلَى الْجَنَّةِ، وَمَا اجْتَمَعَ قَوْمٌ فِي بَيْتٍ مِنْ بِيُوتِ اللهِ يَتْلُونَ
كِتَابَ اللهِ وَيَتَدَارَسُونَهُ بَيْنَهُمْ الا نَزَلَتْ عليهِمُ السَّكِيْنَةُ، وَ غَشِيَتْهُمُ
الرَّحْمَةُ، وَحَفَّتْهُمُ الْمَلائِكَةُ، وَذَكَرَهُمُ اللهُ فِيْمَنْ عِنْدَهُ، وَمَنْ بَطَأَ بِهِ
عَمَلُهُ لَمْ يُسْرِعْ بِهِ نَسَبُهُ.

EARNING AND SEEKING WHAT IS LAWFUL

An-Nu'man B. Bashir reported God's messenger as
saying, "What is lawful is clear and what is unlawful is
clear, but between them are certain doubtful things which
any people do not recognize. He who guards against
doubtful things keeps his religion and his honour
blameless, but he who falls into doubtful things falls into
what is unlawful, just as a shepherd who pastures his
animals around a preserve will soon pasture them in it.
Every king has a preserve, and God's preserve is the
things He has declared unlawful. In the body there is a
piece of flesh, and the whole body is good if it is good,
and the whole body is corrupt if it is corrupt. It is the
heart.

عَنِ النُّعْمَانِ بنِ بَشِيْرٍ قَالَ: قَالَ رَسُولُ اللهِ صَلِّي اللهُ عَلَيْهِ وَسَلَّمَ:
الْحَلاَلُ بَيِّنٌ وَالْحَرَامُ بَيِّنٌ، وَبَيْنَهُمَا مُشْتَبِهَاتٌ لاَ يُعْلَمُهُنَّ كَثِيْرٌ
مِنَ النَّاسِ، فمَنِ اتَّقَى الشُّبُهَاتِ فَقَدْ اسْتَبْرَأَ لِدِينِهِ وَعِرْضِهِ، وَمَنْ

وَقَعَ فِي الشُّبُهَاتِ وَقَعَ فِي الْحَرَامِ، كَالرَّاعِي يَرْعَى حَوْلَ الْحِمَى

يُوشِكَ أَنْ يَّرْتَعَ فِيهِ، أَلاَ وَإِنَّ لِكُلِّ مَلِكٍ حِمىً أَلاَ وَإِنَّ حِمَى اللهِ

مَحَارِمُهُ أَلاَ وَإِنَّ فِي الْجَسَدِ مُضْغَةً إِذَا صَلُحَتْ صَلُحَ الْجَسَدُ كُلُّهُ،

وَإِذَا فَسَدَتْ فَسَدَ الْجَسَدُ كُلُّهُ، أَلاَ وَهِيَ الْقَلْبُ.

Abu Sa'id al-Khudri told that Abu Musa came to him
and said: 'Umar sent for me to go to him, so I went to his
door and gave a salutation three times, but as he did not
respond to it I went home. He asked what had prevented
me from coming to him and I replied that I had come and
given a salutation at his door three times, but as he had
not responded I went home, for God's messenger had
said to me, "When one of you asks permission three times
and it is not granted he should go away". 'Umar had
asked him to establish the proof of it, so Abu sa'id said
he got up, accompanied him to ' Umar, and testified.

عَنْ أَبِي سَعِيْدٍ الخُدْرِي قَالَ: أَتَانَا أَبُو مُوسَى فَقَالَ: انَّ عُمَرَ أَرْسَلَ

إِلَيَّ أَنْ آتِيْهِ فَأَتَيْتُ بَابَه، فَسَلَّمْتُ ثَلاَثًا فَلَمْ يَرُدَّ عَلَيَّ، فَرَجَعْتُ.

فَقَالَ: مَا مَنَعَكَ أَنْ تَاتِيْنَا، فَقُلْتُ إِنِّي أَتَيْتُ فَسَلَّمْتُ عَلى بَابِكَ ثَلاَثًا

فَلَمْ تَرُدَّ عَلَيَّ فَرَجَعْتُ، وَقَدْ قَالَ لِيْ رَسُولُ اللهِ صَلَّى اللهُ عَلَيْهِ وَسَلَّمَ:

إِذَا اسْتَأْذَنَ أَحَدُكُمْ ثَلاَثًا فَلَمْ يُؤْذَنْ لَهُ فَلْيَرْجِعْ. فَقَالَ عُمَرُ أَقِمْ عَلَيْهِ

الْبَيِّنَةَ، قَالَ أَبُو سَعِيْدٍ: فَقُمْتُ مَعَهُ، فَذَهَبْتُ إِلَى عُمَرَ فَشَهِدْتُ.

SALUTATIONS

Abu Huraira reported God's messenger as saying,
"There are six good qualities which one believer should
display to another: he should visit him when he is ill, be
present when he dies, accept his invitation when he gives
one, salute him when he meets him, say 'God have mercy
on you' when he sneezes, and act sincerely towards him
whether is absent or present".

عَنْ أَبِي هُرَيْرَة قَالَ: قَالَ رَسُولُ اللهِ صَلَّى اللهُ عَلَيْهِ وَسَلَّمَ: لِلْمُؤْمِنِ
عَلَى الْمُؤْمِنِ سِتُّ خِصَالٍ: يَعُودُهُ إِذَا مَرِضَ، وَيَشْهَدُهُ إِذَا مَاتَ،
وَيُجِيبُهُ إِذَا دَعَاهُ، وَيُسَلِّمُ عَلَيْهِ إِذَا لَقِيَهُ، وَ يَشْمُتُهُ إِذَا عَطَسَ، وَيَنْصَحُ
لَهُ إِذَا غَابَ أَوْ شَهِدَ.

PART V

TEACHINGS

CHAPTER 5

Aspects of Islamic Teaching

EQUALITY IN ISLAM

Islam considers that all human beings are equal. There is no difference between them because of their race, colour or tongue. All of them, belong to one family and come from one origin.

This was not the case before Islam came to the Arab Peninsula. Before Islam each tribe considered its members to be superior to those of other tribes, and this made life very difficult between them. They could not deal with each other properly, and they led a difficult life; there were continuous severe fighting between the tribes of Arabia because of their attitude towards each other. Might was right, so the weak had practically no rights.

When Islam came, it was a long step towards correcting the attitude of Arab people, and making them aware of their brotherhood with others. The poorer people and the humbler tribes were quick to follow the Prophet because they saw in Islam a hope of leading a good life, for in Islam they heard something they had never heard before. The voice they heard gave them hope that people could live as equal human beings.

But at the same time, their accepting Islam was a reason for the leaders of the tribes to object to the call of the Prophet, because it was hard for them to consider these weaker people as their brothers. But the Prophet (peace be upon him) made it clear from the beginning, as the Holy Qur'an says:

'O men, we created you from a single pair
of a male and a female, and made you into nations
and tribes that you may know each other, and
not that you may despise each other.
Verily, the most honoured of you in the sight of
God
Is he who is the most righteous of you
And God has full knowledge
And is well acquainted with all things'.

The Prophet himself emphasized this by his action, and his behaviour, by treating all human beings as his equals, even his slaves.

There is an interesting story about this. It is related that the Prophet's wife, Khadija, had a slave called Zaid, whom she gave to the Prophet to help him with his personal affairs. The Prophet treated him as his own son, and the youth never felt he was a slave. According to the law of Arabia before Islam, when war broke out between two tribes, the winner could take the women and children of the defeated tribe as slaves. Zaid had become a slave on one of these occasions, and he moved from one hand to another until finally he reached the hand of the Prophet. His father and uncle were looking for him everywhere. At last they discovered that he was in Makkah with the Prophet Muhammad, and they went to Makkah and asked the Prophet to return Zaid to them. They offered the Prophet whatever he wanted as ransom for the Boy. When the Prophet heard this, he called Zaid to him and said: "This is your father, and this is your uncle'.

Zaid recognized them, and said he knew who they were. The Prophet said:

> *'If you want to go with them, you are free to go, and if you want to stay, you are welcome to stay'.*

The Prophet left the choice with the boy, and what Zaid answered astonished his father and his uncle: Zaid refused to go with them, and said to the Prophet:

> *'I will never prefer anyone to you, not even my father'.*

His father and uncle were surprised and annoyed, and said:

> *'What are you saying, Zaid, do you prefer slavery to freedom?*

'No, said Zaid, 'but there is no-one who could treat me like the Prophet treats me'.

When the Prophet saw that, he wanted to please the father and uncle of Zaid, and he went out in public and announced that Zaid was not his slave, but his and, son that he had a right to deal with him as a son. This shows us the new system the Prophet introduced among Arab people, with equality for each man no matter what his tribe or colour.

Once he was speaking on Hajjat al-wada, (farewell pilgrimage). He said,

> 'O people, all of you are children of Adam, and Adam was created form dust. No Arab is superior to another, but in righteousness, and there is no superiority for anyone above another because of his race or colour of tongue. All of you are equal'.

This is what the Prophet said in the last year of his life to stop discrimination between human beings. The only time that man is raised in the sight of God is when he offers good deeds and gains a pure heart. The Prophet says, 'Allah doesn't look at your pictures or your faces, but at your hearts and your deeds'. Muslim people carry on this message after the Prophet.

At the time of Omar Ibn al-khattaab,the second Caliph, at season of pilgrimage, while Jabalah of Ghassan, the last king of the Ghassan family, was doing Tawaf around Al-Kabah, a Bedouin who was walking behind him trod on the king's train. The king got angry and turned towards the Bedouin and struck him in the face. The Bedouin went to Omar to complain. Omar called Jabalah, and asked him: 'Did you strike your brother, fom the tribe of Fazarah?'

The king answered,

'He is not my brother. I am a king and he is a commoner'.

Omar said,

'But Islam created equality between you.'

The king answered sharply,

'Are you trying to say that we are equal- I am a king

and he is a commoner. By Allah, I would have cut his head off, but because of the honour of the House of God I did not'.

'Now that you have confessed that you struck him,' Omar said 'You must give him the chance of satisfaction'.

The king repeated what he had said,

'Are you going to give him the right to punish me- I am a king and he is a common man'.

'It is the law of Islam', Omar said. When the king saw it was the only way he asked for a chance to think of a solution.

This event gives us evidence of how Islam created equality between all human beings, and because of this teaching, Muslims were able to establish Islamic civilizations in a short time, and to offer great benefit to all mankind.

At the end of this subject, I must refer to what is happening in countries like America nowadays. They cannot find a solution to this problem, because the white man has rights the black man does not have. This happens all over the world-but if they want to take a good example, let them turn to the example of Islam.

CULTURE IN ISLAM

Islam lays a great deal of stress on the educational aspect from the beginning, because of its importance in the life of human beings. The first verses of the Holy Qur'an which were revealed ordered the Prophet to read. They say:

'Read in the name of thy Lord,

Who created, created man from a clot of congealed blood.

Read! and thy Lord id most bountiful.

He who taught the use of the Pen

Taught man that which he knew not.'[1]

This leads us to understand that Muslims should gain as much knowledge as they can, because the Holy Qur'an also considers knowledge as light and ignorance as darkness-and considers the knowledgeable man as a live man and the ignorant man as a dead man: and that those who have knowledge fear God most. For Allah says:

"*Those truly fear God*
Among His servants, who have knowledge'.[1]
'The blind and the seeing
Are not alike. Nor are the depths
Of Darkness and the Light.'[2]

There are many sayings of the Prophet which encourage Muslims to seek knowledge from the beginning of their lives until the end, and which also consider knowledge as the way which leads to Paradise.

First he said

'*Seek knowledge from the womb to the grave*',

and he also said:

'*whoever sets foot on the way to knowledge, Allah directs him to the way to Paradise*'.

Once the Prophet entered the Mosque, and found two groups of Muslims sitting there, One of them was occupied in contemplation of God, and the others were studying. He joined the group of these who were studying, and this was a sign that he appreciated their way and encouraged Muslims to seek knowledge by any means. In another Hadith he said:

> 'The angels spread down their wings in appreciation for the seeker of knowledge'.

The Prophet not only gave verbal encouragement to people to seek knowledge but took every chance to provide opportunities for a large number of people to learn to read and write, as this is a way to knowledge. This is clearly illustrated after the Battle of Badr, when the Muslims took a number of prisoners from Quraish in the battle. Some of them were literate. The ransom of those who could read and write was that they should teach ten Muslim children to read and write.

When you read the Holy Qur'an you will find many verses urging Muslims to study what they see around them on earth and society. They cannot use them rightly unless they have some knowledge, and the knowledgeable people are of high rank in the sight of God-for the Holy Qur'an says;

> "Those who know and those who do not know cannot be regarded as equal'.[1]

In other parts of the Qur'an which deal with the story of Adam and the Angels, we are told how God informed the Angels of the creation of Adam, and they asked how this could be, and suggested that maybe the new creation would do wrongs, whereas the Angels only glorified God. But when they met Adam they knew that his knowledge

was greater than theirs because God had taught him things
that the Angels did not know.

> 'Behold, thy Lord said to the Angels:
> 'I will create a vicegerent on earth.' They said
> 'Wilt thou place therein one who will make
> mischief therein and shed blood?
> Whilst we do celebrate Thy praises
> And glorify Thy holy (Name)?
> He said 'I know what ye know not'.
> Of all things; then He placed them
> Before the Angels, and said, "Tell me
> The nature of these if ye are right'.
> They said, 'Glory to Thee; of knowledge
> We have none, save what Thou
>
> Has taught us; In truth it is Thou
> Who art perfect in knowledge and wisdom'.
> He said, 'O dam tell them
> Their natures'. When he had told them
> God said 'Did I not tell you
> That I know the secrets of heaven
> And earth, and I know what ye reveal
> And what ye conceal?"[1]

The Muslim people understood clearly the approach
of Islam towards education. Therefore they started to gain
knowledge, taking the guidance of the Holy Qur'an as a
light to show the right way. And therefore they established
Islamic civilisations which prevailed throughout most of
the world, and gave human beings the benefit which they
got from the teaching of the Holy Qur'an, and the history
of Islam is full of famous Muslim thinkers in every branch
of knowledge: philosophy, law, science, astronomy and
art.

THE POSITION OF WOMAN IN ISLAM

People nowadays talk a lot about the position of women in Islam, particularly Western people, who believe that women have no rights in Islam comparable to those enjoyed by European women. Such criticisms surprise Muslim scholars, and they wonder how Western people arrive at this idea about the status of women, since it is completely contrary to the facts.

The woman in Islam has full rights in the same way that man has. No difference at all exists between male and female, except when it comes to physical duties which a woman cannot perform, or financial responsibilities, which rest completely on the shoulder of man. To understand this further, we have to study what the Holy Qur'an says and what the Prophet Muhammad taught regarding the status of women in Islam. In the Holy Qur'an we find that when God speaks to the believer, he always says: 'O you who believe, male or female'. This kind of address always occurs in the Holy Qur'an, and it illustrates that both sexes are treated equally.

Sometimes, however, a woman is exempted from certain duties on physical grounds, such as the duty of fighting to protect one's country, and of earning a living for the family. To develop this point further, woman in Islam, whether she is a daughter or sister, a wife or mother or grandmother, has no responsibility to maintain or support herself. This duty falls to the man. If she is a daughter, her father is responsible for her, if a sister her brother is responsible; if a niece an uncle; if a wife, her husband. If she is mother, a son is responsible for her, if a grandmother, a grandson. This responsibility, has been prescribed by the law of Islam and if and Muslim tries to escape from fulfilling his duty, the judge in Islam has a right to take what the woman needs by force from his assets and give it to her. If he continues to neglect his duty the judge is empowered to order the deduction of the required money from his income. This protection is granted to the woman so that she can lead a good life. If we compare this situation with the rights of a European woman, we will find a big difference. Once a girl in Europe has reached the age of 16 her father is not legally responsible for her any longer. If her father refuses to supply her needs, she is obliged to make her own way in life, and many women advanced in years have to go out to work in order to live. Such a situation in Muslim society would be a source of shame and scandal to the members of the family.

A woman in Islam is entitled to buy and sell and involve herself in any business she chooses, as long as her actions will not affect her honour, and she is entitled to use her money for her benefit through any agency or directly, and no one has a right to take this money from her, whether he is her husband or her father, unless she gives it to them voluntarily. Furthermore a woman in Islam will keep her maiden name after marriage, and this illustrates the amount of independence she still retains and within marriage. In the case of European woman, it is customary for her to assume her husband's surname.

Some people refer to the right of inheritance in Islam, and use it to illustrate that woman has less rights than man, but if we bear in mind the great responsibility borne by the man and the fact that the woman bears no responsibility, we will realize the wisdom of giving a man double the rights of inheritance to those accorded to a woman. Suppose a man died and left two sons and two daughters, then his legacy will be divided into six parts each girl will receive one part and each son will receive two. It may sound unfair if we forget the man's responsibility towards the woman, but if we remember the duty of the son to spend his own money in keeping his sisters and in providing them with a suitable home until they get married, we will realize why Islam gives the man a double share in the inheritance.

Marriage and divorce in Islam are regarded by some Western people as being very different in that a woman is treated as being second class. But if we understand the system of marriage in Islam we will come to realize that this is not so.

Marriage in Islam is very important, and Islam does its best to support and protect family life and to save it from any breaking. Thus a man and woman have both the right to know about each other before getting married, with regard to the standards of the family, the character of its members, their way of life and also to know what the prospective spouse looks like. The woman has every right to refuse anyone who has come to propose marriage to her if she does not wish to accept him as her husband. No one can force her. Her word is the final word, even if her father has previously given his word. The following example will show us attitude of Islam towards this particular point from time of the Prophet.

A man once decided to marry his daughter to his nephew.

The daughter came to the Prophet and said:

'O Messenger of God-my father has decided to marry me to his nephew so that his position in society may be enhanced.'

The Prophet said:

'It is up to you to accept what your father has decided for you or to refuse'.

The girl said:

'I have accepted what my father decided for me but I only wanted women in Islam to know that a man has no right to force her choice in marriage'.

HOW TO ESTABLISH A FAMILY IN ISLAM

Islam knew well the effect of the family in the future of the nations. As we have said before, the family is the foundation of society. If it is strong, it will be good, but if there is anything wrong with it, this will cause trouble in the society. For that reason, Islam gave much care to the family. Also, when we study its teachings, we find emphasis upon husband and wife to treat each other in the right way.

Islam advised the husband through the Prophet Muhammad (blessing of God and peace be upon him) when he said: "Do what is best for the women for they were created from the rib. It is necessary always to lead her with gentleness and tact and not to use force or brutal ways".

This is because Islam made men and women equal and gave to the woman as it gave to the man, especially in the case of marriage, because the Arab people married their girls against their will. When Islam came, it gave the women freedom of choice. For example, a girl once came to the Prophet and told him that her father had made her marry his brother's son. Then The Prophet said: "It is for you to refuse". But she answered: "I accept my father's decision but I should like other girls to know that they cannot be forced to do anything against their will".

And not only this. He also made it clear that the good man is he who is the kindest and most helpful to his family. The messenger of God said: "The best and noblest man amongst you is he who is kind, benevolent and helpful to his family. I am the best possible example on this subject, therefore follow me".

The Prophet also made it clear that a good wife is the best thing a man can have in this world when he said: "The best thing for a man after keeping his duty to God is to have a good wife. When he looks at her, he is happy and when he makes a request, she obeys him. When he is absent from home she will certainly keep his money safe and his honour intact". May be this is one of the reasons why Islam called upon all Muslim people to put religion first when choosing whom they want to marry. As the Prophet said: "Favour her who has a good religion. Islam made the perfect organization of the family".

For example, Islam divided the duties of husband and wife to give them the chance to help each other, as they can do. The duty of the husband is to earn money to keep himself, his wife and children and to look after her and provide her with food and clothing. The wife, in turn, organizes and runs the household and looks after the children. Listen to what the Holy Qur'an says about this subject: "Men are the protectors and sustainers of women because God has given the one more strength than the other and because they support them by their endeavours".

May be you remember what we said before, that Islam gave us clear advice in marriage. It called upon us to be sure of the morals and behaviour of the man or woman because the result of the lives we live are passed on from the parents to the children.

Islam knew well the effect of heredity and environment on the offspring. The Prophet Muhammad (blessing of God and peace be upon him) said: "Choose with thought for you offspring. The children inherit all things from their parents." He also warned us against the girl of low morals, even if she is very beautiful, with these words: "Take care not to marry the girl who has a beautiful face but lives among bad, ill-tempered people; she is like a rose in the dirt".

All this shows the great care which Islam gave to the family, before and after marriage, so that the family would live under peace, co-operation and love. May be this is the meaning which the Holy Qur'an wished us to understand from this verse: "That He created mates for you from among yourselves that you may dwell in tranquility with each other, and He has put love and mercy in your hearts for those who reflect". And when the Holy

Qur'an reviews the graces that God has given to his servants, the wife was one of them. Listen with me to what the Holy Qur'an says on this subject; "God has made for you mates and companions of you own nature, and made for you out of them sons and daughters and grandchildren and provided you with the best sustenance".

HOW TO CHOOSE A WIFE IN ISLAM

Islam paid a great deal of attention to the family because the family is the foundation of society. If it is strong, the society will be strong; if there is something wrong with it, then this will cause trouble in the society. For that reason, Islam gave much care to the family.

The family starting with husband and wife:

They will start anew life together with new responsibilities. The co-operation, love and understanding of each other are all Necessary to make a happy and successful married life. This is the meaning of the verses in the Holy Qur'an which says:

> "And among His signs is this, that He created mates for you among yourselves that you may dwell in tranquility with them, and He put love and mercy in your hearts for each other. Verily in that are signs for those who reflect".

When we try to know how Islam paved the way for a man and woman to establish a happy family it will be clear that this is the right way for human societies to get what they need for a happy life. Islam called upon the Muslim people to give a great deal of thought to whom they wished to marry, the man to think about the girl, the girl to think about the man. The man must be sure that he knows everything about the girl. As she will be a great influence upon his future, It is good for us to listen to what the Prophet Muhammad (blessing of God and peace be upon him) said about this situation. As we know, Islam encouraged the young men to marry when they could because it wished to safeguard the society from any trouble. The messenger of God said:

"O group of young men, whoever can must marry",

and he also said:

"Marriage is my way. Whoever does not like my way is not among my followers".

One of the teaching of Islam in this instance is to be sure to really look at the girl whom you wish to take as a wife. When one of the Prophet's companions wanted to marry, he said to him:

"Go and look at her. It is proper for you to be on friendly terms with each other".

When people wish to marry, many of them prefer one who has a great deal of money or who comes from a good family or is good-looking, but Islam advised the Muslim people to look for the qualities of good conduct and high morals and strong faith. The Prophet Muhammad said: "Men favour a woman for her riches, her family, her beauty and her religion, but most important is to put her religion first.

Islam also knew the effect of heredity and

environment on the children, and that instincts, sentiments and character are passed on from parents to children. For this reason, the Prophet ordered us to be careful when we choose a wife. He said: "Choose with thought for your offspring, for the children inherit all things from their parents". He also warned us against the woman of low morals even if she is very beautiful. "Do not marry the woman who has associated with those of bad temper, Or ill character. She is like a rose among the dirt". We also know from the sayings of the messenger of God that we must be sure about the religion and morals and religion, he will treat his wife instructs him to do. The Prophet said these words to fathers: "Whoever comes to you for permission to marry, if you accept his religion and his morals then accept him as a husband for your daughter".

Let us take another example:

Once a man came to Al-Husain Ibn Ali and said: " I have a daughter; to whom do you think I should marry her? Husain replied: " Marry her to he who fears God; if he loves her, he will treat her well, but even if he doesn't love her, he will never treat her with injustice".

HOW TO BRING UP CHILDREN

Our duty towards our children in this country is very great. We should look after them, educate them and give them a good chance to have perfect knowledge, real faith and good treatment and straight behaviour. Our children need much from us, and a great deal of attention, especially under the difficult circumstances of their lives in their country. There is no relationship between the manner of life here, and the teachings of their religion. Our responsibility is, indeed, great and God will surely ask us about it. I do not know how we can answer if we have neglected our duty. The saying of the Prophet is very clear: "Everyone of you is a ruler and everyone of you shall be questioned about those in his care: The woman is a ruler in her husband's house and she shall be questioned about those she has in her care: the servant is a ruler as far as the property of his master is concerned, and he shall be questioned about that which is entrusted to him.

One of the greatest responsibilities is to be just between your sons and not allow yourselves to favour one above the other. This will surely cause trouble between them and corrupt the good relationship between their hearts. May be we can understand this more fully by listening to the following:

One of the companions of the Prophet called Alnuman Ibn Bashear said: My father gave me a gift, but his mother, Amra Bint Rawaha did not agree that he should accept the gift until he had made the messenger of God a witness. So the father came to the Prophet and said: "I gave a gift to my son, but his mother has bidden me to make you a witness, O messenger of Allah". The Prophet replied: "Have you given the same to all your sons? " The father said that he had not. Then the Prophet Said: "Be careful of your duty to Allah and practise justice between your children". Then the father turned and took back the gift".

The Holy Qur'an gave us an example when we listen to Luqman's advice to his son: " Behold, Luqman said to his son by way of instruction: O my son join not others on the worship of God; for false worship is indeed the greatest wrongdoing. (We have enjoined on man to be good to his parents: in travail upon travail did his mother bear him, and in years twain was his weaning: hear the command: show gratitude to Me and to your parents. To Me is the final goal. But if they strive to make you join in worship with Me things of which you have no knowledge, obey them not; yet bear them company in this life with justice and consideration and follow the way of those who turn to me in love. In the end all of you will return to Me, and I will tell you the truth and meaning of all your doings).

"O my son," said Luqman, "if there be but the weight of a mustard seed and it was hidden in a rock or anywhere in the heavens or on the earth, God will bring it forth: for He understands the deepest mysteries and is well acquainted with them. O my son establish regular prayer, enjoin that which is just and forbid that which is wrong, and bear with patient conduct of affairs. And be not puffed up with pride, nor walk in insolence through the earth; for God loves not the arrogant boaster.

And be moderate in your pace and keep your voice low, for, without doubt, the harshest sound is the braying of the ass".

When we consider the advice of Luqman to his son, we learn the foundations of the good life and correct education. They are faith in God, right treatment to others, good conduct and perfect knowledge. It is our duty to give these to our children, but these things are also essential for a strong society, a happy life and secure future.

The father who does this for his children will certainly have a good reward in this life and in the life to come. The Prophet (blessing of God and peace be upon him) said: "When a man dies all his deeds are finished except three things; his charitable works, his works of knowledge and a righteous son who Prays for him".

Goodword English Publications

The Holy Quran: Text,Translation and Commentary (HB), Tr. Abdullah Yusuf Ali

The Holy Quran (PB), Tr. Abdullah Yusuf Ali

The Holy Quran (Laminated Board), Tr. Abdullah Yusuf Ali

The Holy Quran (HB), Tr. Abdullah Yusuf Ali

Holy Quran (Small Size), Tr. Abdullah Yusuf Ali

The Quran, Tr. T.B. Irving

The Koran, Tr. M.H. Shakir

The Glorious Quran, Tr. M.M. Pickthall

Allah is Known Through Reason, Harun Yahya

The Basic Concepts in the Quran, Harun Yahya

Crude Understanding of Disbelief, Harun Yahya

Darwinism Refuted, Harun Yahya

Death Resurrection Hell, Harun Yahya

Devoted to Allah, Harun Yahya

Eternity Has Already Begun, Harun Yahya

Ever Thought About the Truth?, Harun Yahya

The Mercy of Believers, Harun Yahya

The Miracle in the Ant, Harun Yahya

The Miracle in the Immune System, Harun Yahya

The Miracle of Man's Creation, Harun Yahya

The Miracle of Hormones, Harun Yahya

The Miracle in the Spider, Harun Yahya

The Miracle of Creation in DNA, Harun Yahya

The Miracle of Creation in Plants, Harun Yahya

The Moral Values of the Quran, Harun Yahya

The Nightmare of Disbelief, Harun Yahya

Perfected Faith, Harun Yahya

Bouquet of the Noble Hadith, Assad Nimer Busool

Forty Hadith, Assad Nimer Busool

Hijrah in Islam, Dr. Zafarul Islam Khan

Palestine Documents, Dr. Zafarul Islam Khan

At the Threshold of New Millennium, Dr. Zafarul Islam Khan

Islamic Sciences, Waqar Husaini

Islamic Thought..., Waqar Husaini

The Qur'an for Astronomy, Waqar Husaini

A Dictionary of Muslim Names, Prof. S.A. Rahman

Let's Speak Arabic, Prof. S.A. Rahman

Teach Yourself Arabic, Prof. S.A. Rahman

Islamic Medicine, Edward G. Browne

Literary History of Persia (Vol.1 & 2), Edward G. Browne

Literary History of Persia (Vol.3 & 4), Edward G. Browne

The Soul of the Quran, Saniyasnain Khan

Presenting the Quran, Saniyasnain Khan

The Wonderful Universe of Allah, Saniyasnain Khan

A-Z Ready Reference of the Quran (Based on the Translation by Abdullah Yusuf Ali), Mohammad Imran Erfani

The Alhambra, Washington Irving

The Encyclopaedic Index of the Quran, Dr. Syed Muhammad Osama

The Essentials of Islam, Al-Haj Saeed Bin Ahmed Al Lootah

Glossary of the Quran, Aurang Zeb Azmi

Introducing Arabic, Michael Mumisa

Arabic-English Dictionary, J.G. Hava

The Arabs in History, Prof. Bernard Lewis

A Basic Reader for the Holy Quran, Syed Mahmood Hasan

The Beauty of Makkah and Madinah, Mohamed Amin

A Brief Illustrated Guide to Understanding Islam, I.A. Ibrahim

The Concept of Society in Islam and Prayers in Islam, Dr. Syed Abdul Latif

Decisive Moments in the History of Islam, Muhammad Abdullah Enan

The Handy Concordance of the Quran, Aurang Zeb Azmi